A Rising Wind

BOOKS BY WALTER WHITE

A Rising Wind
The Fire in the Flint
Flight
Rope and Faggot

WALTER WHITE

A Rising Wind

DOUBLEDAY, DORAN AND COMPANY, INC.

Garden City, New York

1945

For my son
WALTER
with the prayer that his generation,
white and Negro, may be wiser
than was his father's

At the close, Mrs. Roosevelt quoted a phrase from the late Thomas Wolfe, ending, ". . . a wind is rising and the rivers flow."

"Yes," she said, "a wind is rising throughout the world of free men everywhere, and they will not be kept in bondage. The rivers flow in the democracies that now exist through to those who are held temporarily in slavery and on to the deluded human beings who are voluntary slaves.

"They have thought that force and cruelty and people who cast aside free choice and accept the will of one man or a few men can endure and dominate. But the rivers flow so swiftly they cannot be turned back, and the new beds which they make for themselves are in the pattern of new ideas which the people who believe in freedom in the world are fashioning today. Democracy shall triumph."

The New York *Herald Tribune*, September 29, 1941

A Rising Wind

Chapter One

———————◆———————

"WE WISH you'd come over for a look-see," a Negro Red Cross worker in England wrote. Between the lines of the censored letter there was more to be read than in the lines themselves. Rumors—some good, most of them bad—had come back to the United States of relations between white and Negro American troops. One had told of a distinguished British family inviting a group of American soldiers to their home for dinner and dancing. Everything moved smoothly during the meal, but when one of the Negro soldiers danced with one of the Englishwomen, he had been assaulted by a Southern white soldier. A free-for-all followed in which the British took the side of the Negroes.

And there was the story of the pub keeper who had posted a sign over his entrance reading "THIS PLACE FOR THE EXCLUSIVE USE OF ENGLISHMEN AND AMERICAN NEGRO SOLDIERS."

But how to go? Civilian travel being banned, the choice seemed to lie between going as an official observer, which would entail some restriction of movement and publication, or as a war correspondent. There were some people in the War Department and a few Army officials in the European Theater of Operations who were none too keen to have the facts investigated and published. But their opposition was overcome in time. Assistant Secretary of War John J. McCloy, Undersecretary Robert P. Patterson, Brigadier General Alexander Surles, chief of the Bureau of Public Relations, and others believed that there might be some value in an appraisal and possible recommendations which would help to ease, if not to solve, the tough problem created by Americans who, fighting a war to defeat a master-race theory, had transplanted to other parts of the world the racial patterns and prejudices of Mississippi.

The New York *Post* requested my accreditation as a war correspondent, and that request was granted. A few weeks later, credentialed, uniformed, inoculated, briefed in the use of Mae West belts, and a little scared, we took off from an East coast airport, enveloped by all the necessary secrecy of such wartime departures. As we sped northward over peaceful New England towns and villages, it was almost impossible to believe that a war was raging or that the C-54 in which we were flying would soon be a possible target for enemy planes as we winged over the ocean. We were due at a Newfoundland base in late afternoon. But when we reached our first and only stop, we did not descend, but circled above the airport for an hour. A soldier came out of the cockpit and crisply told us, "Fasten your seat belts as tightly as you can. We've got to make a very fast landing." Upon landing we found the ground crew had been certain we would never make it in the teeth of a forty-five-mile gale blowing straight across the runway. My respect for the skill of ATC fliers was born at that moment and steadily mounted thereafter.

Toward midnight we took off again. Snugly fastened into my Mae West belt, I fell asleep. Awakening, an Air Corps colonel pointed to land far below on our right. "It should be on our left," I remarked. "That's the tip of New-foundland, isn't it?"

"No, that's not Newfoundland; it's Ireland!" was his astounding reply. In the space of a sound sleep we had flown the Atlantic. Though I had read often of others doing so, it was a jolt to have experienced the virtual demolition of time and space.

And then I thought, why should I be surprised? In a sense, wasn't that what this whole trip was about? In the old days, when time and space were material obstacles, the world could afford separate racial and national compart-ments. At least such an arrangement was possible. Now England was less than a score of hours from New York; India sixty hours instead of sixty days from Manhattan; Africa but little farther than England. And here I was on my way to probe the transplanting of racial emotions and patterns from Mississippi to the Midlands. Men had used creative genius to demolish the space between the areas of the earth. But the same instruments were being used to transport prejudice and hate. It made one neither comfort-able nor hopeful of the kind of world we were building.

General Eisenhower was just about to be transferred from the North African Theater of Operations to England to prepare for the invasion when I reached London. Gen-erals, colonels, majors, captains, and lieutenants were jittery. No one knew whether he would remain in England for the big show or be sent elsewhere. Each was so concerned with his own fate that there was little time or inclination to discuss what would seem to him only a small segment of a far greater problem. Brigadier General Tristram Tupper, chief of the Public Relations Office, to whom war cor-respondents were responsible, was about to be shifted to

North Africa. He provided me with an escort to meet Lieutenant Colonel Lawrence, already selected to succeed General Tupper.

It was late afternoon; shadows were deep in the long, narrow room. A trim military figure was silhouetted against the window. My escort, a captain, snapped his heels together smartly and saluted the Colonel Lawrence I was about to meet. A deep voice rumbled out of Colonel Lawrence: "Walter, what the hell are you doing over here?" As we drew near, I found that Colonel Lawrence was my old friend, Jock Lawrence, of Hollywood. And at that moment I knew that my path would be smoother.

A day or so later he made arrangements for me to meet his chief, Lieutenant General John C. H. Lee, chief of SOS, and destined later to be made deputy theater commander of the European Theater of Operations. General Lee told me of the spots where there had been racial clashes and of some where the difficulties had been averted. He issued orders to commanding officers that I be given opportunity to see whatever I wished. He assigned as my escort Captain Max D. Gilstrap, former science editor of the *Christian Science Monitor* and then associate editor of *Stars and Stripes*. Captain Gilstrap comes from Oklahoma. Our driver was also a Southerner—Private Moore, who comes from the Eastern Shore of Maryland. I never failed to get enjoyment out of hearing Private Moore ask for "petrol" in an accent redolent of Chesapeake Bay.

Thus started our peregrinations around ETOUSA—the European Theater of Operations, United States Army—which Max described in an inscription in a book he presented me many weeks later: "In memory of the weeks we rode the range together in England!"

Chapter Two

"THE LIBERTY CLUB, near the British Ministry of Information," I told the taxi driver.

He looked at me, believing me to be white. "You mean the Rainbow Club of the American Red Cross, don't you, sir?" he asked.

On being assured I wanted the Liberty Club, he exclaimed, "Oh, I know now, sir; you mean the American Red Cross Club where the black boys go."

The club was formerly a middle-class hotel, a well-arranged and, on the whole, attractively equipped one. It was Saturday afternoon and the place was filled with men on leave from the London area and near-by towns. The snack bar was crowded with hungry GIs, among them several white soldiers; the Georgia accent of one of them was thick as the mud of the Chattahoochee. He told me he preferred the Liberty Club to the Rainbow or any other "white" Red Cross club in London because he had made friends with several colored soldiers whom he couldn't meet comfortably in other clubs. I asked him about the continuation of these friendships when he returned to America. Ruefully he spread his hands, palms upward, and shrugged his shoulders. "I don't know," he said sadly.

During the afternoon and evening strange tales were told

me. One of the men had been sent with his regiment to a famed British university town. They were the first Negro troops in that area. During the initial days they fancied there was a note of apprehension, mingled with curiosity, in the attitude of the townspeople. If one of them was walking on an unfrequented street, men and women noticeably crossed to the other side of the street. Children hid behind their mothers' skirts, peeping out curiously. Some of them even forgot to ask the question that has become a byword during the American occupation in England: "Got any goom, Yank?"

After a few days they began to learn the reason why they were shunned. When word had come that Negro troops were to be moved into the region, white American troops had told the townspeople that Negroes had tails, that they were illiterate, that their color was due to disease, that all Negroes carried razors which they would use on the slightest provocation, and that "they will rape your women." Some of the more imaginative ones had told the British, "These Negro soldiers wearing the American uniform are not like your colonials. They are just some savages we picked up in Africa to do manual labor here."

At that time there were virtually no Negro combat troops in ETOUSA. The time was a half year before D-Day. Approximately one tenth of the huge number of Americans in the theater were Negroes. One group was an anti-aircraft battalion with eight mounted anti-aircraft guns which guarded a supply depot. All the other Negroes in the European Theater served in engineer, quartermaster, trucking, or port battalion units. Seeing Negroes do only manual labor in most of the small towns in England, Wales, North Ireland, and Scotland, where no Negro had ever before been seen in the flesh, credence was at first given by uninformed Britishers to some of the fantastic stories about Negroes which were being spread.

One soldier gave me a mimeographed copy of an official order which an American colonel of Southern birth, since promoted to the rank of general, had issued. In it were paragraphs such as these:

That colored soldiers are akin to well-meaning but irresponsible children. As such they have to be given the best possible care by their officers and at the same time be subjected to rigid discipline. Generally they cannot be trusted to tell the truth, to execute complicated orders, or to act on their own initiative except in certain individual cases.

That among the peculiar characteristics of the colored race . . . influences such as excitement, fear, religion, dope, liquor, or the accomplishment of something without their usual sphere, they individually or collectively can change form with amazing rapidity from a timid or bashful individual to brazen boldness or madness or become hysterical. . . . The colored individual likes to "doll up," strut, brag, and show off. He likes to be distinctive and stand out from the others. Everything possible should be used to encourage this. For example, know their names and occasionally call a man "Corporal John" in place of "Corporal Smith."

The same soldier showed me an order issued by General Dwight Eisenhower in September 1942, of a very different sort:

. . . The presence of Negro troops in this theater creates a problem of inter-racial relationships much different from that existing in the United States. There is practically no colored population in the British Isles. Undoubtedly a considerable association of colored troops with British white population, both men and women, will take place on a basis mutually acceptable to the individuals concerned. Any attempt to curtail such association by official orders or restrictions is unjustified and must not be attempted. Furthermore, it must be realized by all ranks that it is absolutely essential that American officers and soldiers carefully avoid making any public or private statements of a derogatory nature concerning racial groups in the United States Army. The spreading of derogatory statements concerning the character of any group of United States troops, either white or colored, must be considered as conduct prejudicial to good order and military discipline and offenders must be promptly punished. In the interest of military efficiency, if for no other reason, isolated incidents of friction must be eliminated.

As we talked, I was puzzled at the frequency, despondency, and bitterness of the use of the phrase "the enemy." I soon learned that Negro soldiers referred not to the Nazis across the Channel but to their white fellow Americans. One of them, his face clouded with disillusion and anger, asked me, "What are we fighting for over here? Are we sent to the ETO to fight the Nazis—or our white soldiers?" Having then listened for four hours or more to recitals of transplanted American race prejudice, I had no answer to give him.

During the afternoon and evening I talked with men from eighteen or twenty separate military installations. With the exception of those in the London area, there was unanimity among the men in resenting the "off-limits" rule established by commanding officers to avoid clashes not only between white and Negro American soldiers but, in some instances, between white Americans on the one hand and Canadian, French, Polish, and British on the other, when soldiers of these countries championed the cause of Negroes being mistreated by American whites. Here is how the "off-limits" rule was used. When white and Negro troops were billeted in the same area, commanding officers would declare town "X" as out of bounds for Negro soldiers and town "Y" for white soldiers. In sparsely settled regions, where there were few towns, and most of them small, recreational facilities consisting usually of only a pub or two and a moving picture theater, a system would be set up for whites on "odd" nights and Negroes on "even" nights. Facilities for diversion being already sorely limited, both whites and Negroes resented this further restriction.

But all the tales were not dolorous. A sergeant was on that day enjoying his first visit to London although he had been overseas for eighteen months. He told me a story of what had happened in a charming town in the Midlands which I later visited. The first American military installation in that area was a salvage and laundry unit. Here American efficiency manifested itself at its best. GI clothing, shoes, and other equipment were sent to this town from all over the ETO. The clothing, after being washed, sterilized, and repaired, was put into use again at a great saving to taxpayers. Most of the units are mobile. So, too, are vehicles for the repairing of shoes and making of corrective footwear.

Because most of this work was done by Negroes, the first Red Cross unit in the town was established by a Negro Red Cross worker. He was a handsome man of deep brown skin, and carried himself with great dignity. He came from Denver, Colorado. Nazi bombers had destroyed many buildings in the town. Military needs of the British and American armies had pre-empted virtually all other available quarters. Only one building was available—the home of a banker for which various war and civilian agencies vied. But the personality of George Walton, the Red Cross director, had so favorably impressed the banker that he got the house.

The sergeant told me how a few white soldiers then in the area had at first ignored the club; then had gone by ones and twos to look at it and promptly leave; and eventually had found there a place of friendship and comfort. The first real test came a few weeks later, when a large contingent of white American soldiers, most of them from the South, was moved into the area. The commanding officer was also a Southerner. He gathered his men together on the first afternoon to tell them bluntly that the only Red Cross club in town was run by a Negro director and staff; that any soldier of his command who objected to such an arrangement should not go to the club; and that if any of his soldiers caused any trouble, he would be promptly court-martialed. There was no trouble.

Later an airdrome was constructed near by, bringing a greatly increased number of American soldiers. When I visited this Midlands town, I was told by the mayor and other citizens that, whenever an American soldier had drunk more than he could stand, he would tell whomever he met, "Get me to the Red Cross Club and Mr. Walton will take care of me."

And then there was this added item told me by the sergeant. The Red Cross proposed to open another club in the town—this one "for whites." Not only did the townspeople protest, but so did the white American soldiers.

Almost without exception, the brightest note in the stories of all Negro soldiers I talked with that afternoon was the story of friendships they had formed with the British people. At first alarmed by the tales about Negroes, the British common man had reacted in favor of those who he believed had been maligned and against those who had told stories about Negroes which the British have found to be fantastic and untrue.

There are interesting facets in the reasons for these friendships. Away from the sophistication of cities such as London, Liverpool, and Edinburgh, the British in the smaller towns are a simple, friendly people with a passion for fair play. But the bond between them and American Negroes was not based on abstract principle or indignation against an injustice. The overwhelming majority of American soldiers, white and Negro, are also decent human beings, not given to flamboyant boasting or rowdy behavior. But some soldiers made no attempt to conceal their contempt for towns and people which did not have all of the mechanical gadgets which are commonplace in the United States. The absence of telephones and radios, electric refrigerators and vacuum cleaners to most soldiers of this type denoted an inferior civilization and a backward people. When such opinions were loudly and frequently expressed within earshot of the British, they made no contribution to Anglo-American amity.

The average weekly income of more than 60 per cent of the British people is three pounds, ten shillings—or about fourteen dollars at the rate of exchange during the war. More than three fourths of the Negro troops in England early in 1944 came from the South—another area of depressed income. They, like the British, were not so accustomed to highly mechanized gadgets. Therefore they were not so prone to derogatory comments upon British living as were some of their white fellow Americans. So, too, did somewhat better manners restrain them from giving offense. Learning this in time, the British developed respect and friendship for Negro soldiers which they, in turn, cherished. For many of the Negroes it was their first experience in being treated as normal human beings and friends by white people.

The administration of justice by American courts-martial to Negroes was frequently shocking to the British people. Unfamiliar with the psychology of many Americans, particularly those from the South, when Negroes were charged or suspected of sex offenses, they could not understand the rapidity and casualness with which Negroes were convicted. Typical of this reaction among the so-called common people of England is the following letter from an Englishwoman, moving in its simplicity and its quiet recital of the preparation of the appeal by the writer's husband and the circulation of a petition in support of appeal even though "the German bombers at that time were paying us some attention. . . ."

SIR:

Please pardon the liberty I take in writing you. We are concerned at the unjust sentence passed on Joseph Ballot, a young American Negro soldier, who was stationed here in Portsmouth.

He was arrested in February last while on his way to camp about twenty minutes before midnight.

The arrest was made because a girl said she had been molested. There was no evidence to prove this, for at the trial neither the girl nor the policeman recognized the young man. Yet he was sentenced for natural life; no doubt on account of his color.

The people of Portsmouth were horrified at the sentence and suggested something be done. My husband prepared an appeal. I obtained 276 signatures and could have got many more had I the time. The German bombers at that time were paying us some attention and we were afraid the list might get destroyed, for some men wanted to take it into the dockyard and another to a factory.

People in all walks of life talked about the injustice of the sentence.

My husband sent the appeal with an accompanying letter through military channels. We got no news.

I then wrote to General Eisenhower, who referred my letter to the B.G. of ETO [Brigadier General of the European Theater of Operations], who more than ever confounded us by saying the lad had been sentenced for rape. There had been no mention of this at the trial. It was supposed to be attempted assault.

All that happened to the girl was something to the face, whoever was guilty.

Sexual desire is not confined to the Negro soldier. Every young person, no matter what rank or color, is liable to succumb to the desire.

Crime should be punished, but let there be justice for all.

We are asking ourselves why we stood up to the nights of terror in 1940 and 1941 if it was not for the freedom, justice, and rights of all men?

We are hoping most sincerely that you will be able to do something for this unfortunate young man.

All that we have accomplished is to get the sentence reduced to twenty years.

A white American sailor, tried for murder, received a sentence of only ten years!

With all good wishes from the citizens of Portsmouth.

An editor of a London weekly, who is also a member of Parliament, sent me recently an account of a similar case which he had printed in the *Tribune*. Mr. G. R. Strauss, the editor and member of Parliament, prefaced the verbatim account of the trial of the Negro soldier with the statement, "We print it in full even at this critical stage of the war because one of the purposes for which our men are fighting is the defense or restoration of the dignity and equality of all individuals—whatever their color or creed—even amidst the tumult and chaos of our day," and adds in his letter, "The whole question of imposing death penalties on American soldiers in this country for crimes which are not punished by death sentences under British law is being raised in Parliament."

The evidence in the case was so contradictory that General Eisenhower personally investigated the case, countermanded the sentence of death, and restored the Negro soldier to duty.

Whether justified or not—and I found some instances where Negro soldiers have been fairly tried and properly convicted—there was a general belief among Negro soldiers, many British citizens, and some white American soldiers and officers that the court-martial procedure was upon occasion used to break the spirit of Negro soldiers, particularly those who knew their rights and insisted upon exercising them. Such soldiers were considered by some of the officers to be "radicals" or "troublemakers." This was particularly believed to be true of special courts-martial where a single officer acted as judge, usually dealing with less serious offenses for which the maximum penalty is six months. General courts-martial, where several officers made up the Court of Inquiry, were usually found to be more attentive to the form and procedure of weighing the evidence and meting out justice. I examined the records in a considerable number of courts-martial.

One of the most startling was the case of a Negro sergeant. A white captain of Military Police had addressed Negro soldiers as "niggers." Two of the soldiers drafted and circulated a petition to their commanding officer, vigorous but respectful in tone and content, in which they pointed out that Army regulations forbid the use of epithets or mistreatment by an officer of men under his command.

The two privates were court-martialed and sentenced to ten years at hard labor. The sergeant, who had not signed the petition, wrote a letter of protest to the commanding general through channels, asking that the sentences be reviewed because the convictions had materially lowered the morale of the Negro soldiers. When no reply was received to this communication, the sergeant wrote directly to the commanding general of the base section, which is a violation of Army regulations. It was for this crime that he was convicted and sentenced to six months' imprisonment at hard labor, forfeiture of twenty dollars per month pay, and reduction to the rank of private.

Chapter Three

‎————◆—◆————

"IT LOOKS PRETTY GOOD, but it's still spiced ham," said General Lee as he passed hors d'oeuvres in his London flat. Just at that moment air-raid sirens burst forth with their blood-chilling shrillness. "We arranged that specially in your honor," General Lee said, smiling.

Joining us at dinner were key officers in the various Army services. Colonel Roy Lord, now Brigadier General Lord, chief of staff of the SOS, was there. Colonel James Franey, deputy chief of staff, Jock Lawrence, Colonel Solbert, chief of Army Special Services, and others connected with the vast and intricate Army organization joined in the discussion of the coming invasion, of American versus British methods, of the problems created by some of the white soldiers in their attitudes toward Negro soldiers.

"We know there are a lot of things wrong here in ETOUSA," General Lee said. "We know that we've handled some of them badly and unintelligently. But we are going to open up every office to Mr. White so that he can see and appraise the facts for himself. All we ask is that he in return tell us about the things he thinks are wrong and give us an opportunity to correct them."

Succeeding weeks produced ample evidence that the promise of every opportunity to see whatever I wished to see and to talk with whomever I wished under circumstances of my own choosing was not merely after-dinner oratory. Later I asked permission to look over correspondence and directives dealing with the subject. I was permitted to do so. In them I found much that was heartening, much that was disheartening. Orders unequivocal in their emphasis had been issued by the top-ranking officers—by General Eisenhower, Lieutenant General Jacob L. Devers, and Lieutenant General Lee—that all soldiers wearing the uniform of the United States Army be accorded equality of treatment. Subordinates were ordered to act promptly and vigorously to prevent discrimination.

But there were other orders and directives in the files issued by subordinates. Some ordered or suggested establishment of "off-limits" or "out-of-bounds" towns and areas of cities. Others suggested various means of evading or negating compliance with the explicit commands of their superiors.

Especially significant were documents revealing the official attitude of the British Government. During the early days of the American "invasion" the British Home Office had issued a directive to all constables and peace officers throughout the United Kingdom, bluntly reminding them that "There is no color bar in the United Kingdom and none will be permitted" unless it is established by the United States Army in the areas under control by the United States Army. Constables were told sternly that under no circumstances were they to participate directly or indirectly in the barring of American Negro troops from any place of public accommodation.

This order was issued after a succession of "incidents," among them the barring from a London hotel of Leary Constantine, West Indian cricketer, who is regarded by the

British cricket-loving public as Babe Ruth was a few years ago by the American baseball fans. Constantine, his wife, and two children were requested to leave "by a high official of the Ministry of Labour" after Americans had objected to his presence in the hotel. The incident was hotly debated in the House of Commons. Eleven members of Parliament joined in raising the issue on the floor through parliamentary questions directed at the Government. One of the questions, by R. F. Bower, a Conservative, demanded to know of Mr. Bevin whether the action of the official of the Ministry of Labour had been taken with his approval. A Labour member, R. W. Sorenson, proposed that racial discrimination against colonial subjects be made illegal. Tom Driberg, Independent, proposed that the Ministry of Food should take over control and administration of establishments attempting to impose a color bar.

The British press joined in the campaign. David Low, internationally famous cartoonist, drew a series of hard-hitting, ironic cartoons for the widely circulated London *Daily Mirror*. In one of them an American Negro soldier and a turbaned Indian soldier pass a hotel on which hangs a sign, "No colored people admitted. By order." In the caption beneath, the Negro soldier, pointing to the sign, exclaims, "We didn't see *that* notice in the trenches."

In another cartoon, which Low labeled "British Empire Hotel, Colonel Blimp, Manager," signs were posted reading "No dogs or natives," and "Hitler race theories. Please take one," the latter affixed to a stack of books, presumably *Mein Kampf*. In the foreground a walrus-mustached proprietor is shown ejecting a well-dressed Negro carrying a cricket bat bag. The proprietor is saying "Gad, sir, we can't have a colored man here. It would take the minds of resident stinkers off their struggle for the ideals of the British family of free and equal peoples."

The raising of the issue in Parliament and the press appears to have materially decreased the number of incidents of this character. But more and more Americans were pouring into ETOUSA. In a quiet way the Army was taking steps to inoculate American soldiers against behavior of this character. Lectures were given aboard ship en route to England, reminding soldiers that they were not to manifest whatever prejudices they might have. An excellent film, *A Welcome to Britain*, starring Burgess Meredith, was hastened to completion to be shown to all soldiers in the European Theater. It explained in a simple, friendly fashion the difference between British and American habits, customs, money, and ways of life.

In the film was included a brief but pointed sequence warning against race prejudice. Meredith and a Negro soldier were shown emerging from a railway carriage. Each searches his pockets in vain for cigarettes. The Negro soldier goes to a newsstand, purchases a package, and shares it with Meredith in a normal, friendly fashion. At this point Meredith in an aside comments upon an Englishwoman having invited the two soldiers to tea. Effectively and engagingly he tells the soldier audience that such courtesies are frequent and normal in England and warns them that for the sake of winning the war as speedily as possible they must abandon whatever prejudices they may have brought from America. At this point Meredith spies General Lee, who urges the same attitude.

I overheard an interesting reaction to this film in a preview at the Curzon Cinema, at which I was the only American present. Back of me sat a British general and another

British Army officer. Just as the episode preaching racial tolerance was completed, the general exclaimed in surprise to his companion, "Why, they *are* doing something about the question after all!"

But in the meantime other and different influences were being brought to bear on the British Government. Most of the clashes between white and Negro troops had occurred when white soldiers physically resented the association in public of British people—particularly women—and American Negroes. These clashes occurred not only when Negroes associated with women of easy virtue, such as the "Piccadilly Commandos," but also when there was association with British women where there was no element of sex involved. An order was later issued to all commanding officers of British units, especially to commanders of ATS, WRENs, and WAAFs. The first section of this order consisted of a highly condensed history of the Negro in the United States, stressing the fact that he had been a slave for two and a half centuries in the United States (but not mentioning the part British slave traders had played in that trade) and emphasizing the social distinctions between Negroes and whites which were a part of American life.

The order then proceeded to "suggest" that, since some American whites resented any association of white and colored people, members of the British military units, especially British service women, should refrain from associating in public with Negroes. "This does not preclude entertainment of Negro friends in your homes or other private places," the order concluded.

One evening Herbert Agar and I were the only two Americans at a London dinner party. The conversation continued to return to the new patterns of race relations which were being imported to and spread throughout England. At times the resentment against Americans coming to England and presuming to tell British men and British women with whom they could or could not associate reached the point of indignation.

When Agar and I mentioned India we were impressed with the fact that nowhere in the thinking of our dinner companions was there any connection whatever between the American attitude toward Negroes whose skins were black or brown and the British attitude toward Indians whose skins were brown.

Just before the dinner ended I sought to bring into the conversation that there might be some connection.

"It is my hope to visit India on this trip," I remarked. "I have been told by Lord Halifax and the India Office that Lord Wavell would receive me at the Viceregal Palace at New Delhi. But if Lord Wavell and I should go from New Delhi to Calcutta and he wished me to dine with him at the —— Club, there might be some difficulties." The guests looked at me with astonishment.

"Why should it be embarrassing?" demanded one of the guests who had been most vehement in criticism of American race prejudice.

"Because the —— Club boasts that no person of colored blood has ever crossed its threshold. And I am a Negro."

There was no further discussion that evening of the race question.

It was suggested that I talk with General Alexander regarding my itinerary before leaving London. He had been charged with the responsibility of investigating and correcting conditions where there had been friction between Negro and white soldiers. A veteran of World War I, with the soft speech of his native Virginia, General Alexander received Max Gilstrap and me one Sunday afternoon in an office into which crept the heaviest pea-soup fog I had ever seen in London.

"If we could close up Piccadilly Circus for the duration our problem would be solved," General Alexander remarked. "Because most of the trouble is caused by women who run after Negro soldiers because they can get more money out of Negro soldiers than they can from whites."

It seemed best not to discuss this until I had made my own investigation and secured the facts.

"The answer is segregation," he continued.

"And have you found any instances where Negro and white soldiers were not segregated and yet got along together without friction?" I asked him.

He told me that he had found one such instance in Devon. When asked what he had done about that situation, he answered, "I ordered separation because I knew there *would* be trouble."

The British are constantly agape at the miracles of production of war materials, the transportation of them through waters infested with submarines, the distribution and super-efficient handling of supplies by the American Army. One day I was taken through a huge building constructed in large part from the packing cases in which planes and tanks had been shipped from America. The building was piled to its ceiling with equipment for field or base hospitals. From that building could be supplied every article from operating tables to bandages for the setting up of a 450-bed field hospital or a 750-bed, 1000-bed, or a 2000-bed base hospital. I asked the officer in charge how long it would take to set up a 2000-bed hospital and have it in operation.

"Seventy-two hours at the most," he replied with quiet pride. "All we need is a building, doctors, and nurses."

Another miracle whose benefits we appreciated even more in what was then a theater of preparation was the officers' mess in the swank West End hotel, Grosvenor House. From a balcony at street level, stairs on either side descended to what had formerly been the largest skating rink we had ever seen. The assembly-line method of feeding was raised here to its ultimate perfection. For two and one-half shillings, or forty cents, one could secure a tray generously filled with meat, two vegetables, salad, bread and butter, and dessert. Waitresses served as much coffee, cocoa, or tea as one wished. On each of the 250 tables were huge jars of peanut butter and jelly.

Inevitably this officers' mess was soon dubbed "Willow Run." It became the counterpart of Broadway and Forty-second Street and the Café de la Paix, where one, if he waited long enough, was sure to meet every person he knew and get a cross section of opinion on every conceivable subject.

Max and I frequently ate at Willow Run and would purposely direct the conversation to the question of Negro-white Army relations. It was an interesting and profitable exercise. If our companions happened to be men like Ralph Ingersoll, former editor of *PM*, or Major Lawrence Cramer, former governor of the Virgin Islands and also former director of the President's Committee on Fair Employment Practice, or C. D. Jackson, former *Time-Life* editor and now of the OWI, we learned much because of their knowledge and interest in the subject.

But very frequently we talked with less well-informed officers who told us stories which were sometimes hair-raising. We discovered that there had been an almost complete transference of the American pattern of racial attitudes to English soil. We heard contemptuous references to

British people who ignored the color line and invited Negroes to their homes. Not infrequently did we hear the word "nigger" or, among the slightly more educated, "nigra."

Because I did not want in any way to jeopardize Max's position as an officer of the United States Army, I most often sought to sample opinions of this character when I ate alone at Willow Run. I was to learn later, by comparison, that the incidence of race prejudice seemed to be considerably higher among officers, although they were, as a rule, better educated, than among enlisted men. I was repeatedly impressed and depressed by the fact that a nation which could work such physical miracles of production, transportation, and organization to wage war was unwilling to use as much of that energy and determination to tackle the social, political, economic, and racial causes of war. This was emphasized by the ease with which long-held prejudices were dissolved or minimized among the more intelligent when fellow officers presented factual material to explode those prejudices.

Chapter Four

AN INTERESTING CONTRAST between white officers and enlisted men was presented one afternoon when, at the request of a sergeant, I attended a bull session with a group of enlisted men who wanted to talk about the race question. There were between eighty and ninety crowded into every available spot of a sizable room. All were dressed in dungarees, having just come from a near-by park in the West End of London. The highest-ranking officer among them was the sergeant who had invited me. When drafted, he had been teaching at a well-known school for poor whites in the mountains of north Georgia.

"We are men from all over the United States," he said in his introduction. "Most of us had given little thought to the race problem before we entered the Army. But over here we are beginning to realize that the race problem is not confined either to the South or to the whole United States —that it is a world-wide one to which we've got to find a solution. The reason we asked you to come and talk to us is that we feel you will tell us the truth." With that, he sat down on the floor with the others.

I talked informally about the global, the national, the sectional, and the Army aspects of race. I told them of Félix Eboué, black Governor-General of French Equatorial Africa, whose decision in 1940 to refuse to follow Vichy into collaboration with the Germans had played a decisive role in eventual recapture by the Allies of control of the Mediterranean and the Middle East, without which victory Hitler might have long since won the war.

When I finished, questions were fired at me with the directness and almost with the rapidity of .50-caliber bullets from the wing of a P-51. A soldier from Detroit shot the first question at me. He wanted to know what had so radically changed his native city as to make possible a race riot of the magnitude of the one of June 1943.

"It looks quite different from over here," he said. "Don't the people back home realize that they are playing Hitler's game?"

I tried to explain to him how subversive organizations like the National Workers League, the Ku Klux Klan, and followers of men like Gerald L. K. Smith, Father Coughlin, and the Rev. J. Frank Norris had successfully utilized anti-Negro prejudice in building up organizations which they hoped would eventually gain control of Detroit. He was gravely disturbed. "What's the use of fighting over here while we lose democracy at home?" he wanted to know.

It was from another soldier, this one from the South, that I heard for the first time of German prisoners of war being fed in comfort in a restaurant of a town in his native state, while wounded American Negro soldiers en route to a hospital had been made to go around to the back and eat in the kitchen. Before he left home, he told me, he would have thought nothing of this. But overseas he was shocked at the behavior of those with whom he had formerly lived and agreed.

Another Southerner told us about the shock he had experienced when, shortly before being shipped overseas, he had gone to the Stage Door Canteen in New York City and found colored hostesses and servicemen participating just like everyone else. It made him so angry that he had left the Canteen, but, because it is a place where most servicemen who are strangers in New York gather, he went back several times and suddenly found that it no longer bothered him. "If we can play together, why can't we fight together?" he asked. When I told him of the proposal that had been repeatedly made to the War Department to end segregation by establishing at least one voluntary division and opening it to men of all races, he exclaimed, "I'd like to be the first to volunteer. Then I wouldn't feel like a God-damned hypocrite when people over here ask why, in fighting a war for democracy, the United States sends over one white and one Negro army."

The questions of social equality and intermarriage had not been raised up to this point. But now it came. I expected the usual disagreement. Again I was surprised by the unanimity of opinion that every human being should have the right to choose his own friends and associates.

The hour we had scheduled grew into two and then to nearly three. As we broke up, one man demanded to know why the Army did not include in its indoctrination courses facts about race which would enable men to understand the full implications of the race problem before the world, because of its blindness, stumbled into war.

It is not contended that this group is representative of the American Army overseas, nor even of a majority of American servicemen. It would be fortunate for America if it were so. But that afternoon and on many other occasions it was impressed upon me that America is losing the greatest opportunity it has ever had to re-educate ten million or more of its men and women in social understanding. I do not mean that they should be propagandized. Timidity characterizes virtually every approach. Fear of criticism from unintelligent and reactionary members of Congress or from the press and organizations of like character had dominated government action on these issues.

Some weeks later I encountered the same reaction in a field hospital close to the Cassino line. It was in March when the Germans had stopped the Allies cold. From the vantage point of Mount Cassino German guns poured death upon Allied troops in the valley below. Shattered, bleeding bodies poured into the tent in a gory parade. One of the doctors, an American, told me, "Whenever a French soldier is brought in here, his first question is how soon will he be well enough to return to the front. But when an American soldier is brought in his first question is usually whether or not his injury is sufficient to have him sent home." The doctor's startling remark caused me to try to find an answer. Some of the obvious reasons, of course, were that Americans entered the war later, they had not seen their own cities bombed and invaded, and most Americans still believe that an ocean on either side of the United States provides eternal protection. But it was already beginning to be clear that there were political and social factors in the thinking of a distressingly high percentage of American soldiers for which they were not altogether to blame. The same pattern was found in all other theaters.

Besides the reasons already mentioned, others began to be apparent. One was seen in comparing the reading matter, and particularly the service newspapers, of the various Allied armies. *Stars and Stripes* is a sprightly and unusually well-edited newspaper. But its editors, many of them highly skilled newspapermen, had learned from bitter experience that it would be dangerous to permit publication of any "controversial" material. In contrast, *Union Jack*, British servicemen's paper, and *Maple Leaf*, journal of Canadian troops, included in virtually every issue one or more informative articles regarding jobs, housing, political and economic systems of the postwar world. Controversy and dissent were encouraged rather than tabooed, with the result that British and Canadian and, to a somewhat more limited extent, Australian, New Zealand, French, and Polish soldiers manifest greater interest in and knowledge about the causes of the war and the nature of the postwar world than do American soldiers.

A similar situation exists in the respective Army bureaus for the dissemination of knowledge to troops. The United States Army Special Services Division is directed by many men of vision and great ability. But they, too, are sorely restricted to subjects which are "safe." Some of the *Army Talks* are excellently conceived and written. But many of the commanding officers and their subordinates consider the Special Services publications as being so much "hogwash."

The British ABCA (Army Bureau of Current Affairs), on the other hand, bars virtually nothing of importance in their literature and discussion groups. The courses given by ABCA are an integral part of the training of British soldiers, as much as those in the use of firearms and the flying of planes. The results can be seen by anyone spending an hour with a group of British soldiers and then one with a comparable American group.

But, taken individually, American soldiers reveal themselves with gratifying frequency to have developed opinions of their own. One day John Dierkes, then of the American Red Cross, brought me a letter written by Private John Stevens Sweet, of Granville, Ohio. John is white. Michael Powell and Emerich Pressberger of Archer Films, Ltd., had seen him in a soldier performance of *The Eve of St. Mark* by Maxwell Anderson. They sought him out after the performance to ask him to play the role of an average American soldier in a film they were then casting, *The Canterbury Tale*. The story is a simple, unpretentious one of four people meeting in the ancient cathedral tower. They come gradually to realize that past and present are one as time and human emotions are measured. Sweet is a tallish, gentle American, with a homeliness more impressive than the prettiness of any Hollywood star. If he is the average American, America's destiny is secure.

When *The Canterbury Tale* was finished, Sweet wrote a letter to his commanding officer. He wrote the letter because, though his means are modest, he wished the compensation he was to receive for appearing in the film to be devoted to the most effective means of implementing the ideals he had personified in *The Canterbury Tale*.

. . . Steeped in the traditions of Ohio [he wrote], which has a long history of service on behalf of the Nation, and as a firm believer in the democratic rights of minorities, he [Sweet —in the third person of Army memoranda] feels that payment for any work he does would be most appropriately used for the furtherance of these ends, and especially since the money is earned for the portrayal of a typical, democratic American.

Sweet's commanding officer and his superiors were agreeable. His compensation was turned over to two organizations he named which devote themselves to the cause of the Negro.

Captain Perkins was a pastor of a Negro church in Virginia. His manner seems at first deferential. Later one knows that the proper adjective is not "deferential" but "dignified."

For weeks, as Max Gilstrap and I drove through the country, I listened hour after hour to Max in a high tenor voice imitating Chaplain Perkins singing the obbligato of a spiritual, "I Can Tell the World."

More than a hundred engineer, quartermaster, and trucking soldiers working in camps in the same area got together, under the stimulus of Chaplain Perkins' enthusiasm, twice a week to sing for their own amusement and sense of comradeship. It helped them to forget the long hours of toil in mud and cold. It helped them to forget the cruelty of some of their white fellow Americans. By word of mouth, the fame of the singing group spread. They sang at near-by camps and soon, under the skilled leadership of Chaplain Perkins, they became an integrated concert unit, skilled in audience reaction. Albert Hall was engaged and Roland Hayes was brought from America as soloist. It caused a sensation. Even the stolid British burst into tears and cheers. Of that performance Ambassador John G. Winant said to me many months later, "It was one of the two or three great emotional moments in a man's life, if he be fortunate."

Chaplain Perkins, at the request of General Lee, arranged a special concert for our party. It would be difficult to imagine a less concertlike atmosphere or scene. We had been forced to drive furiously after blackout to reach the Army camp in East Anglia in time for the concert. There was no moon or stars; no dying fragment of light in any house we passed; all road signs had been removed throughout the area during the 1940–41 blitz. Time and again we got lost but eventually, hungry and weary, we arrived.

The chorus was to sing in a huge Nissen hut. The only heat was supplied by two British stoves about the size and shape of a short length of stovepipe—one almost literally had to sit on such a stove to know that there was heat coming out of it. Everyone was dressed in mud-stained work clothes. The men moved about in the uncertain light cast by a few undersized electric-light bulbs, trying to keep warm. The commanding officers of three near-by camps had joined Colonel Hallock, who commanded the engineering unit stationed at the point where the concert was held. Mufflered and gloved and trench-coated, we sat sipping coffee which Chaplain Perkins had thoughtfully provided when he found that we had missed dinner. But once the men began to sing, we forgot even the hot coffee. Because there was no orchestra, Chaplain Perkins apologized, the chorus would not be able to sing "A Ballad for Americans" or two Bach chorales which had been sung in London; they could sing only unaccompanied numbers. If there has ever been a more magnificent singing than there was that evening, none of us had heard it. Forgotten were the dampness, the crude benches, the gnawing of hunger; forgotten even was the war. Each of us was caught up in a moment of superlative beauty amid the perils and discomforts of war. Problems of race and combat and physical comforts were forgotten.

It was too late to leave for our next destination when the concert was over. Somehow, somewhere, Chaplain Perkins found army cots for the five in our party; these he arranged like the spokes in a wheel, the center of which was a round-bellied and red-hot American stove which drove out the damp. From mysterious tin cans and other receptacles mixed up with hymnbooks and Bibles and magazines and other implements of his calling, Chaplain Perkins produced cold sliced chicken and chocolate bars, crackers and cheese, cigarettes and cookies. As we were about to go to sleep, we told him, in answer to his inquiry as to what we wanted to have for breakfast, that we would settle for nothing less than steak. At breakfast we *had* steak—sliced from the stewing beef for the camp's luncheon.

But in his generosity, which seemed to give him as much pleasure as it did the recipient, we began to understand how the morale of the soldiers who knew Chaplain Perkins and other men like him was kept alive in the face of segregation and humiliation which ate deep into the hearts and minds of Negro soldiers.

Not all of the Negro chaplains, unfortunately, worked as courageously and devotedly for the welfare of their men as did Chaplain Perkins. Some of them are dubbed "Uncle Toms" by Negro soldiers because of their eagerness to appease prejudiced white officers and take the easiest road for their own advancement. Some of them were lazy. But an incalculable service has been rendered by chaplains like Captain Perkins. It is they to whom a large measure of credit should go for the extraordinarily fine conduct of Negro troops who have set a pattern of behavior in the face of provocation which would have caused many men to riot.

Chapter Five

———◆———

AMERICANS who before the war knew East Anglia from the North Sea just south of Scotland down to the Channel ports would hardly recognize it today. The face of this part of England has been completely changed by American Army engineers and engineer troops. In the space of a few months airdromes were built at phenomenal speed for the use of a mounting tide of American-built bombers and fighter planes. Some airfields were also constructed for the British. Tremendous camouflaged depots were erected, some of them almost overnight. Farms, wooded areas, and even villages were taken over to provide the land for these installations.

It was early January, when the English dark remained until nine o'clock in the morning and returned at four-thirty in the afternoon. Our first stop after leaving London was at an airdrome under construction. Colonel Thompson, the commanding officer, and the mixed staff of Negro and white officers drove their men at an unbelievable pace. Such speed was necessary. The Germans had resumed their almost nightly bombing of London and of the east coast of England shortly after I reached London. It had been stepped up to a furious pace in an effort to postpone as long as possible the invasion of the Continent. British and American engineers were learning more and more about the robot bombs and other "secret" weapons the Nazis were preparing to use. In a steadily increasing number RAF planes by night and American bombers and fighters by day streamed across the Channel to blast German industrial centers and rocket-bomb installations in the Pas de Calais region. Sometimes the airdromes being built for British and American bombers would be bombed by the Germans even before their construction had been completed. Colonel Thompson showed us a huge section of a 6000-foot runway which had been destroyed by a German bomb almost before the concrete had hardened.

After luncheon Colonel Thompson assembled the men of his command in a large metal hut. To permit the men to talk freely, the colonel had tactfully suggested that he and all other commissioned officers should absent themselves from the meeting. Two reactions were immediately noticeable among the men: one of apprehension that reprisals of a vague but terrifying nature would inevitably follow any honest expressions of opinion; the other a devil-may-care attitude to show other fellows that the speakers were not afraid.

An example of the latter was a fiery assertion by one of the soldiers that he and the other Negroes in his unit were being forced to work from dawn until after dark and that this was true only because they were Negroes. I directed his attention to the white engineer unit located close by and asked the hours that unit worked. He stood thoughtfully for a moment in silence; a titter which grew into a roar of laughter swept over the audience. The soldier resumed his seat.

But many of the complaints were wholly justified. "If the War Department believes I can best serve in an engineering unit," said one soldier who, I learned afterward, held a master's degree in mathematics from the graduate school of the University of Michigan, "I am willing to serve there. But it hurts to see all Negro soldiers over here restricted to manual-labor units. It's pretty tough identifying oneself with a war when all he does is dig ditches in the cold and mud. If only we knew there were some Negro flyers, artillerymen, and fighters, as well as service troops, over here, we'd feel better."

Others spoke of refusing passes or furloughs because they knew that if they went into town it would be difficult to avoid unpleasant experiences with white troops. Another soldier, who had been brought up and educated in a Northern city where his companions had been both white and Negro, wanted to know why, if America and her Allies were really fighting for democracy, he should be thrust into a segregated unit.

The restrictions placed upon war correspondents in an active theater of operations were only a small part of the handicap I faced in attempting to answer these questions, for there was no answer. But I could not help wishing that the policy-makers of the Army and of the United States Government had been there also to answer the questions of this kind which not only these men but many white soldiers as well, asked; for in the nearly three thousand miles of travel by staff car, jeep, plane, train, and other vehicles I was met by the same queries everywhere. They are questions which are going to be asked and which will require honest answers when those who survive return home after the war.

When, later, the absence of Negro combat troops was called to the attention of the Supreme Allied Commander, General Eisenhower, he recognized immediately the justice of the complaint. Upon his request, the War Department sent units of the Negro 92nd Division to the European Theater. In a greeting to the wartime conference in Chicago of the National Association for the Advancement of Colored People, General Eisenhower cabled, "Negro troops did their duty excellently under fire on Normandy's beaches in a zone of heavy combat and suffered substantial casualties. You may well be proud of the accomplishments of Negro troops." Shortly afterward, in a communiqué from Supreme Headquarters, AEF, two Negro companies were officially commended by General Eisenhower for their work in Normandy. In citing a Negro anti-aircraft balloon battery involved in the invasion on June 6, he said that, in spite of heavy losses, "under artillery, machine-gun, and rifle fire, the battery carried out its mission with courage and determination and proved an important element of the air defense team. The cheerfulness and devotion of its officers and men have been commented on by personnel of other units. This report is most gratifying to me. I commend you and the officers and men of your battalion for your fine efforts which have merited the praise of all who have observed it."

On the same day a Negro quartermaster truck company was cited for landing against intense German opposition. It nevertheless salvaged most of its equipment at once and within three days 90 per cent of its vehicles were operating on a twenty-four-hour basis, a schedule which was maintained for five weeks.

One of the outstanding contradictions among Negroes fighting for a democracy is to be found in the fact that race prejudice makes it necessary for the Negro to fight for the right to fight. Having done so, his achievements are seldom remembered; he must constantly act as his own advocate to disprove the reflections cast upon his fighting by his enemies, or, more often, the failure of historians to record those achievements. At times it is evident that some Americans have a mortal fear lest, given an opportunity to prove his mettle as a soldier, the Negro do so. In the face of odds which are sometimes almost insuperable the Negro has fought valiantly and well in every war in which the United States has participated.

But even greater than the fear of his making good as a soldier was the fear of the Negro as a rival in sex. Here it is necessary to speak bluntly. White American soldiers, particularly those coming from the South, were infuriated when some British women clearly emphasized a preference for Negro soldiers. In letters which had been written on the subject by white soldiers, many of them declared to their fellows that they had made threats of what the writers would do to any and all Negro soldiers back home when the war was over. The writers of other letters were better losers. I remember one of them which the author showed me. "When we reached ———, we found that Negro troops had preceded us. They had cornered all the local feminine pulchritude, such as it is. We white soldiers didn't have a look-in. They are apparently better men than we are."

Not all the relations between American Negro soldiers and English, Scottish, and Welsh white women are on a sexual basis. But many of the white soldiers, particularly officers, so bitterly resented the sight of a Negro soldier walking on the street or sitting in a café or restaurant with a white woman that they were unable to restrain their fury. Many if not most of the racial clashes in England were the results of such incidents.

There were courts-martial and death sentences imposed

upon Negroes on charges of rape. It is possible that there were a few instances of rape by colored soldiers. However, an American Army officer of English birth, stationed in England and in a branch of the service where he had opportunity to know the facts, sharply disagreed with me in my admission that there might have been cases of rape of British women by Negro soldiers. He asserts firmly that there was no single instance of rape by a Negro soldier.

Two examples which bear out this officer's contention are worth mentioning here. A Negro soldier was arrested, court-martialed, and sentenced to death for criminal assault. The complainant was an English housewife. She charged that she and her husband were asleep one night when someone knocked on their door. Going to the bedroom window and looking out, she saw a Negro soldier who asked directions to the road which would take him back to his camp. She stated that she dressed, went downstairs, and, after giving directions, agreed to walk a part of the way with the soldier to insure his taking the right turn. Away from the house, she alleged, the Negro soldier induced her to climb over a stone wall and assaulted her. She stated that she was rescued when her husband, alarmed and suspicious at her absence from the house, also dressed and followed her. The case aroused tremendous interest in the English press and was even discussed on the floor of Parliament. The Negro soldier claimed in his defense that he was no stranger to the woman; that they had had sexual relations on several previous occasions, upon each of which he had paid her two pounds; that on the night of the alleged assault he had been short of funds and was able to pay her only one pound; that she had become angry and had charged criminal assault when her husband came suddenly upon the scene as they were discussing the transaction.

When the case was brought to the attention of General Eisenhower, he ordered an investigation and on the strength of its disclosures not only reversed the court-martial verdict but restored the Negro soldier to full duty.

Another case of similar nature occurred while I was in England. A nurse, engaged to be married to a doctor working in the same hospital, became enamored of a Negro soldier, and, according to him and to other eyewitnesses, he sought for a long time to avoid her advances. When chided by her fiancé for her obvious pursuit of the man, she told him that she was determined to find out for herself what made Englishwomen pursue Negro soldiers.

Unfortunately the Negro soldier did not continue his resistance; he and the nurse were discovered in flagrante delicto. The Negro was convicted of rape and sentenced to death. His case is on appeal at this time.

Even more infuriating to some white American soldiers in England than extramarital sexual relations between Negroes and Englishwomen are instances in which Negro soldiers have married Englishwomen. Such marriages were a matter of concern to higher-ranking officers without race prejudice and even to some of the Negro soldiers themselves. All of them are concerned about what will happen when these soldiers return home with white wives, particularly if the soldiers live in the South.

A white commanding officer told me of the following experience he had had in attempting to intervene to prevent such a marriage. He had called upon the parents of the girl and told them what he thought would be inconvenience and embarrassment to their daughter when she went to the States with her husband. To the officer's dismay, the parents had requested him to leave the house; they informed him that they did not welcome his interference; that the young man in question was the most gentlemanly and the best educated of their daughter's suitors; that they had never met a young man they welcomed more as a son-in-law.

Whether married or not, many American Negro soldiers, responding to an absence of barriers to keep them "in their place" as inferiors, expressed their determination to remain in England, or at least not to return to the United States. With a few one felt that such intentions were understandable escapism from the ghettos in the United States which had proved too much for them. But with most of them one believed it was a normal desire on the part of normal human beings to live normal lives.

It is not intended to convey the impression that the behavior of all Negroes in ETOUSA is exemplary. For example, a brawling Negro port battalion arrived in a west coast English port. It had been necessary to run a zigzag course from America to escape submarines, which at the time were a grave hazard to shipping in the North Atlantic. When the voyage, far longer than had been expected, was ended and life belts, which they had been required to wear twenty-four hours a day, could be discarded, land was a welcome sight. The men attempted, with fair success, to drink in one night all the available intoxicants in the town, including the virtually de-alcoholized "mild" and "bitter." Some of the women they encountered were complacent; some were not. Inevitably there was a highly unfavorable reaction in the town against Americans and, in particular, Negro Americans.

It was fortunate that one of the Red Cross clubs in the town had as its director a gracious and intelligent Negro who had formerly directed a successful boys' club in a Middle Western industrial city in the United States. It was fortunate also that the commanding officer of the port was a levelheaded man. The two went into conference. The Negro Red Cross officer made it clear that neither he nor any Negro approved, or would seek to defend any Negro soldier guilty of misdeed. The guilty were punished. But the malodor of their actions remained.

There served on the staff of the Red Cross Club an Englishwoman who was a musician. She organized a choral group which gave on Christmas Eve, 1943, a concert of Christmas carols on the steps of the town hall. The concert was so successful that the group was invited again and again to sing throughout that part of England. Soon they came to represent the Negro in the minds of Englishmen.

But what might be classified as misbehavior by Negroes was seldom the giving vent to physical urges as in the case of the port battalion. More often "outbreaks" were results of men being goaded until they could stand no more. We visited a picturesque, somnolent little town in Cornwall, shortly after a "riot" had taken place.

According to the official record, Negro soldiers with murderous intent had gained possession of machine guns, which they had set up on the town square and fired upon anyone who was within range. The facts upon investigation turned out to be as follows: The unit had but lately arrived in England. Before moving overseas it had been stationed in the South, where its men had been subjected to all descriptions of Jim Crow. They had been forced to wait for busses into town until all the far greater number of white soldiers in the Southern camp had been accommodated. Frequently passes had expired before Negro soldiers could secure transportation. They had been denied food or drink, called "nigger," and had discovered that the uniform of the United States Army afforded no immunity from insult. Protests and a variety of incidents had caused them to be confined to camp for a number of weeks before going overseas. Arriving in England, they had been restricted for additional weeks, ostensibly because they did not have dress uniforms to wear into town. But white units near by suffered no such restrictions.

When the ban was eventually lifted for a few of the men, they found their problems were not ended. White MPs, particularly if the colored soldiers were in the company of townspeople of the English village, required the colored soldiers to produce not only their passes but their "dog tags" as well. The climate at that time of the year in this village is cold and damp. To get at one's "dog tags" one had to unbutton coat, blouse, and shirt. When this was made necessary by the MPs every few yards, bitter resentment began to well up among the Negro soldiers. One night some of them returned to camp, secured machine guns, returned to the town square, and there set up the guns to open fire on the MPs. No English people or other persons were shot. No MPs were shot except in the legs, clearly proving that, despite their rage, the Negro soldiers did not want to cause loss of life.

But this availed them nothing in the courts-martial that followed. The participants were convicted, some sentenced to death and others to life imprisonment, which terms they are now serving in American prisons.

An interesting side light on the new racial situation in England was learned from Virginia-born Lady Nancy Astor and Lord Astor when Max and I were invited to Cliveden for luncheon. We arrived precisely at twelve-thirty, the hour for which we had been invited. A magnificent fire was burning in the enormous fireplace which occupied almost all of the north wall of the great hall, whose size was such that several full-size suits of armor standing on three-foot-high pedestals seemed tiny and dwarfed. Coats and hats and walking sticks covered a long table, apparently the property of other guests who had arrived earlier. But there were no persons about nor did any appear as the minute hand of a giant clock moved inexorably toward the top of the dial and the hour hand toward one.

Max wandered off to find someone to whom he could announce our arrival, reappearing later at the head of the stairs at the other end of the hall and cupping his hands to his mouth to "Yoo-hoo" at me as from one mountain peak to another far away. As we began to wonder if we had come on the wrong day, a young woman appeared, announcing coolly, "I am Miss Kennedy. Does Lady Astor know you are here?" When we explained our plight, she disappeared to summon our hosts. We learned later that she was the daughter of the former American Ambassador to Great Britain.

Staccato footsteps grew louder down the hall. Lady Astor almost literally burst into the room, brushing past Max, whom she already knew, and came to where I stood by the fireplace. She shook hands, regarded me closely, and exclaimed as her first words of greeting, "You're an idiot!" Having heard of her frankness, I said nothing. "You *are* an idiot," she repeated, "calling yourself a Negro when you're whiter than I am, with blue eyes and blond hair!"

After luncheon she took me into a book-crowded sunroom from which one could look so far over broad rolling acres that the concept of England as a small country seemed a mistake. Bombed London seemed many more than the short thirty miles away from such pastoral and manorial quiet and comfort. Almost destroyed Plymouth, of which Lord Astor is Lord Mayor and which we had visited a few days before, seemed here like a terrible and impossible nightmare.

"We never have any trouble with the good black boys," she told me. "It's the near-white ones who cause the trouble. They're always talking about and insisting on 'rights.'"

Without success I sought to tell her that the darker-skinned soldiers may not have voiced their grievances as had some of the lighter-skinned ones with whom she talked but that there was no difference whatever in their resentment against proscription. She told me of the arrangements she and Lord Astor had made for entertainment of Negro soldiers, but it was quite clear it had been on a basis of segregation, of which she approved. As is quite well known, Lady Astor possesses strong convictions, which she voices frankly and vigorously. With biting wit she told us of her tilts in Parliament with Communist and other critics, of the fallacy of rumors about there being a "Cliveden set," of the changes which must be made in the colonial systems of England and other countries.

But in nothing she said was there any hint of a newer world in which there would be much change from the old one. Patched up here and there, a modest extension of education and health facilities and recompense for labor done to more of the "lower classes," white and black and brown and yellow. But one knew she was convinced that control of the destinies of the world would remain in the hands of those who had held the reins before.

Chapter Six

Some amusing situations developed when stories about Negro soldiers boomeranged. In various towns in the Midlands and East Anglia, white American soldiers had told the natives that Negroes wearing the American Army uniform were savages recruited in Africa who could not speak English and that they barked to communicate their wishes. When Negro troops arrived in these places and heard these stories they were at first angered and then amused. They decided to live up to the reputations given them. Passing Englishmen on the street, they barked gently at them.

The English, belying their reputation among Americans of being slow to catch on to a joke, soon began barking back. It was not long before a bond of friendship based upon a shared joke developed.

It may be wondered why British people should have believed stories so fantastic. But it should be remembered that in an overwhelming majority of small towns in Wales, Ireland, Scotland, and England no Negroes have ever been seen before. In seaport towns like Liverpool, Belfast, and Southampton, Negro, Indian, Lascar, and other sailors of colored races are more familiar. In larger cities like London and Edinburgh the only Negroes to be seen have been either West Indian or African students or distinguished Negro artists like Paul Robeson, Roland Hayes, and Marian Anderson, and variety artists like Turner Leighton. The only knowledge of Negroes that many British possessed was that gained from the ubiquitous American motion pictures. Negroes were there invariably portrayed as improvident, simple-minded, loud-laughing, credulous buffoons or menials, scared of ghosts, inordinately fond of razors, watermelons, and their white masters. Fed for decades on such concepts, it was not strange that the British people who had seen Negroes only as Hollywood had shown them on the screen were ready to accept fanciful stories told by prejudiced whites.

Robin Cruikshank, chief of the American Section of the British Ministry of Information, told me one day that because cultured Englishmen had until the war seen few Negroes except distinguished artists, the English have always held a high opinion of Negroes. He added that since Negro soldiers and American colored men and women of the Red Cross have come in increasing numbers to England, Englishmen have been "deeply impressed with the extreme modesty of behavior of the Negroes, their softness of voice, their gracefulness of movement, and their adaptability to strange customs and surroundings. If any of them happen to think ill of us or our country, they don't reveal it."

The Lord Mayor of a university town told me this story of how Negro troops were first received. He and others were alarmed when word was received that a large contingent of Negro soldiers was being sent to their town. There had been a few American and African Negro students at the university but the Mayor had never met any of them. During the first few days of their presence, the mayor told me quite frankly, he had crossed the street or otherwise avoided meeting any of the Negro troops. But one morning he emerged from a building and almost bumped into one of them. The Negro stopped short to avoid a collision, saying as he did so, "I beg your pardon, sir."

Startled at the soldier's use of English, the mayor engaged him in conversation and learned he was a college graduate, though serving in a quartermaster regiment. The Lord Mayor thereafter made it his business to talk with other Negro soldiers and thereby learned to his astonishment that there were several other college or university graduates and a number of high-school graduates among them. The word spread throughout the town as others had similar experiences. In his town, the Lord Mayor told me, there had never been any trouble caused by the Negro soldiers. "They are better behaved than our own soldiers," he added.

The American commanding officer of the installation near that town and the head of the local Red Cross were militantly active against discrimination. With the Lord Mayor they had arranged for Saturday-night dances and Sunday-afternoon teas in the town hall. When some of the white American soldiers objected to the presence of Negroes at these and other entertainments, the whites were told by the Lord Mayor that if they did not like the arrangements they could remain away. There had been no further trouble on that score.

In a few towns special efforts were made by the British to provide entertainment for Negro soldiers, particularly after it became known that Negroes could not freely use facilities open to white soldiers. There was bewilderment that the United States Government insisted on rigid segregation. There were a few colored soldiers in British and Canadian units. These men are not segregated. The British could not understand why a similar procedure did not obtain in the American Army.

In one town the meager rations of sympathetic townspeople were pooled to establish a clubhouse for Negroes. The original plan had been to open its facilities to all American soldiers as a rebuke to some of the segregated American facilities. That plan had been changed when some of the American officers, possibly well intentioned, had advised the townspeople to establish the club "for Negroes."

But on the gala opening night the event was boycotted by the Negro troops, who resented adoption by the British of the American pattern of segregation. Only one or two soldiers went to the opening. They walked in, looked at the pile of sandwiches made from the food which the townspeople had denied themselves, and walked out without saying a word. When, later, some of the Negro soldiers explained to the British why they had acted as they had, the townspeople understood and agreed that they would have done the same thing under the circumstances.

In Devon a specialized training school for the British Army was turned over to the American Army. A committee, headed by a wealthy American woman married to a distinguished British official, had been organized to provide entertainment first for the British and later for the American noncoms. Facilities for recreation were limited in the small rural town. However, there was a charming club to which guest privileges were made available to the trainees. Later some Negro noncoms were sent to the school for training and they, too, were provided with guest cards to the club. A delegation of white commissioned officers served an ultimatum upon the club that the guest cards to Negroes must be rescinded, particularly for the Saturday-night dances. The committee, following the leadership of the chairman, Mrs. Leonard Elmhirst, unanimously refused to comply with the demands of the American officers. But shortly thereafter the Negro trainees were removed from the school.

For weeks we traveled night and day. We saw port battalions lifting from the bellies of ships vast cargoes of materials completed but shortly after the ships which transported these supplies across the Atlantic were finished. We saw these supplies loaded in trucks by Negro and white drivers and swiftly distributed throughout ETOUSA.

It was in a forest that we came upon what seemed to us the ultimate contradiction in logic. There was a closely guarded section where the detonating caps of shells were tested. White and colored soldiers worked side by side at a task where the slightest carelessness could mean death. After the men had finished their perilous stint and were ready to return to their billets, they were separated according to race—whites climbed aboard one truck, Negroes a separate one. An officer had issued an order forbidding American soldiers of different races to ride in the same vehicle!

And there was the day when we flew for the first time in a Flying Fortress. So closely guarded was the location of this bomber base that natives living fifteen miles from it were unable to tell us its location when we asked directions. The commanding officer greeted us warmly in a soft Southern accent. He told me he had read several articles and one or two books I had written.

"I'd agree with most of what you say," he told me, "except for one or two things. But that is possibly due to my having been born in Georgia. I can't go along with you on social equality; that will never be possible."

We sat together at the head table at luncheon surrounded by the nervous bubbling conversation and laughter of men just out of their teens who faced death daily, and yet there was one note of disappointment—weather had "scrubbed out" that day's flight. The C.O.'s second in command, a twenty-six-year-old Texan, the intelligence officer, a New Englander, the C.O., and I continued our conversation about the means by which conflict could be lessened between the two races in the Army.

Several of the towns near the bomber base had been placed "out of bounds" for white soldiers so that they could be used by the large number of Negro troops in the vicinity. These three men were opposed to the establishment of "off limits" but for another reason—it restricted already limited facilities for recreation for white airmen who needed diversion after bombing missions. Not long before our visit there had been a mission deep into enemy territory where enemy planes and flak had been most trying and destructive. One of the B-17s was pursued by enemy planes and shot down over the North Sea. The crew bailed out and was rescued after long hours in the icy waters. Three members of the crew decided to go down to London to find gaiety which would release the tension.

It is possible that they would have gone to London, anyway, because of the greater variety of entertainment in London. But whatever might have been the case, the train on which they were traveling in the fog crashed into another train standing in a local station. One of the fliers was killed instantly. The spines of the other two were shattered.

The bad weather continued to ground planes. The C.O. invited us to stay overnight. "The other members of your party can stay in the barracks. I'd like to have you share my quarters. I have two nice bunks," the C.O. told me. I laughed, somewhat to his puzzlement. "What's funny?" he asked.

"A little while ago you told me that social equality was impossible," I answered, "but now you are inviting me, a Negro, to be your guest."

It was his turn to laugh. "You're different."

Once again, as it does to every Negro above the level of the white stereotype of a colored person as menial or buffoon, the soft accusation of being "different" was encountered. One ought to be able to rationalize this inevitable product of rigid separation of the lives of human beings living side by side in the same land. But that is not easy to do. The movies, press, textbooks, and even the radio picture the Negro so frequently as an amiable dullard that it is not to be wondered at, perhaps, that a Negro possessing even a tiny bit of education sees it magnified all out of proportion—even more at times than the average white American would do in the case of a visitor from Tibet.

On our return to London, General Lee arranged an appointment for me with General Eisenhower to discuss recommendations I had been asked to make. General Eisenhower received us in his small but comfortable headquarters, at that time located in the West End of London. The entire wall facing his desk was covered with a map of the European battle front, studded with pins and markers on which each day's and almost each hour's movements of the armies were marked. General Eisenhower's questions were blunt and to the point. He made no effort to create an impression and one knew after the first few minutes that he attempted to delude neither himself nor anyone else. He made no pretense of being anything other than a soldier whose sole job is to win the war. Yet one was aware that he was conscious of the social forces which make war or peace.

At times I thought he leaned over backward in his efforts to exclude some of the social implications of his job. He told me of a New York journalist with whom he had had a sharp difference of opinion in North Africa.

"He told me my first duty was to change the social thinking of the soldiers under my command, especially on racial issues. I told him he was a damned fool—that my first duty is to win wars and that any changes in social thinking would be purely incidental. Don't you think I was right?" he asked almost belligerently.

I ventured timidly—so overwhelming is Eisenhower's personality—to tell him that I saw merit in the other man's point of view; that, while wars had to be fought and won, we must not fight them solely for the sake of making wars; that we had to change the patterns of thinking which caused men to fight. He nodded reluctant agreement and changed the subject.

He told General Lee and me of his recent visit home; of how he had been so carefully protected in Washington that only the President and a few of the top officials in the War Department knew of his presence there. His face softened and his voice became tenderer as he told us of the visit to his mother and of the thoughtfulness of the other members of his family when they absented themselves from the room to permit him to spend the first few minutes of his brief visit alone with his mother.

The three of us discussed recommendations which had been made to relieve the racial tensions and conflicts which were impeding preparations for the invasion. Both General Eisenhower and General Lee devoted as much attention to the subject as to any major physical detail of the effort which lay just ahead, looking at it more from the standpoint of winning wars than as social workers. One of the items was the paucity of Negro combat troops. Having served with such troops, Eisenhower was keen to have them as well as service troops in the European Theater. He agreed that, rank being as important as it is in the Army, more Negro officers above the rank of captain, as was the case at the time, were highly desirable for what they could contribute, for the effect their presence would have in raising Negro morale and in inculcating among white officers and enlisted men a higher opinion of Negro officers. Both generals were convinced that the proposal to assign Negro and white MPs in pairs to patrol areas together, particularly where Negro and white troops were billeted in contiguous areas, would allay friction considerably—a proposal which subsequently, when put into practice, proved exceedingly sound. More effective checking on the spreading of derogatory stories and correction of false impressions created among the British, the abolition of paternalism as well as more obvious acts of prejudice toward Negro soldiers by some officers, the institution of refresher courses in the use of firearms for service of supply troops, white as well as colored, the abolition of segregation and discrimination in the Army and such Allied services as the Red Cross were frankly faced and discussed.

From a purely physical point of view the job done in England, North Africa, and Italy by the Red Cross had been admirable. Almost everywhere American troops were stationed there also could be found one or more Red Cross clubs with attractive snack bars, game and writing rooms, dormitories, and facilities for dancing, motion pictures, and other entertainment. In more remote places Red Cross club-mobiles, dispensing free doughnuts, coffee, and chewing gum, brought solace and comfort to our boys. Everywhere the Red Cross clubs were comfortably furnished; in some instances, almost luxuriously.

But the very excellence of the service given by the Red Cross to those in the American uniform caused British, French, Canadian, Australian, New Zealand, and other Allied troops to be quietly unhappy because of the great contrast between their service clubs and those of the Americans. The Red Cross had taken over early in 1944 more than 110 of the largest and best hotels and other buildings in England for their use—60 per cent of the cost of which was charged against reverse Lend-Lease. Allied soldiers recognized that, since the money for the American Red Cross units was due to the generosity of the American public, Americans had the chief right to enjoy those facilities.

It appeared to some, however, particularly Morris L. Ernst, of New York City, who was commuting frequently to England on special missions for the Government, that an extraordinarily fine opportunity was being lost by the exclusion of Allied soldiers from the clubs. In tiny, crowded, bombed England the influx of several million additional persons would have taxed housing and other facilities enormously. Another factor was the great decrease in number of buildings destroyed by enemy bombs. There was even greater confusion and overcrowding. With the exception of a few places like the Balfour Club in London there were no places where soldiers of different nationalities and from different parts of the world could meet and become better acquainted except in pubs and on street corners.

A recommendation was made to General Eisenhower and

Ambassador Winant that consideration be given to the combining of American Red Cross clubs and other facilities with those of the British, Free French, and Canadian, the combined services to be known as the United Nations Canteens. It was felt that this would enable men of all races and nationalities to learn to know each other in pleasant surroundings. In the spring of 1944, General Eisenhower issued an order that soldiers of all the Allied nations should be admitted to the American Red Cross centers and that prices be lowered to meet the pay of the lowest-paid soldier. An American columnist, Drew Pearson, very accurately said that this order "will mean all the difference in the world to harmony between United States and British troops during the invasion."

One could not, however, feel happy that military leaders, charged with the responsibility of waging the most colossal war in history, should be forced to divert their time to correcting dangerous and stupid prejudices which a negligent public at home had allowed to flourish. These two men—and their subordinates—in the midst of a desperate struggle for survival of the democracies had inherited or been saddled with the necessity of doing something to bridge a chasm between men fighting in the same army, against an enemy who was trying to conquer the world by means of the selfsame divisive tactics of race hatreds Generals Eisenhower and Lee were forced to combat.

Again and again General Lee and I attempted to end the conversation, acutely aware of the tremendous pressure of time upon Eisenhower. But each time we attempted to rise from our seats he peremptorily waved us back into them. He pumped us dry, with a succession of staccato questions, of all we knew about the difficulties created between white and Negro soldiers. We were agreed on one cardinal and infallible circumstance: that when the commanding officer of a unit was able, courageous, and obedient to the commands of his superior, whether he agreed entirely with his commands or not, there was no friction or, at worst, a minimum of friction. That where officers, on the other hand, were weak or prejudiced to the extent that they attempted to evade or negate orders that all soldiers must be treated alike without any discrimination, those were the areas where riots and fights and other disorders occurred.

Specific steps were agreed upon, among them the issuance of an order forbidding any future establishment of "off limits" on the basis of race.

In having John G. Winant as war Ambassador to England, the United States is as fortunate as she is in having top-ranking officers like Eisenhower and Lee in the Army. He and Herbert Agar have, in quiet fashion, worked wonders at the American Embassy. Upon several occasions I was permitted to spend long hours in discussing not only the vexing and difficult problem of race but other questions as well with Messrs. Winant and Agar. At the Ambassador's suggestion an unpublicized but exceedingly useful Anglo-American Committee was formed upon which served representatives of civilian and military branches of both nations. There was placed before this committee, for example, the matter of the order issued to members of the British armed services "suggesting" that they abstain from associating in public with American Negroes. In this and other situations it was made clear by the embassy that the overwhelming majority of Americans in England were opposed to racial discrimination and they did not wish the pattern of behavior to be based upon the wishes of the most prejudiced.

Chapter Seven

———◆———

A STRIKINGLY YOUNG Navy ensign and I sat in the crowded waiting room of the airport in northern Scotland. A loudspeaker boomed, summoning us to a briefing on the use of life rafts. We were then permitted to go in search of food. Returning, we were briefed a second time about the possibility of a hazardous flight ahead of us. The nervousness of the ensign visibly increased. When at long last we were ordered to the plane, I was glad to see that only half of the bucket seats were occupied by passengers because the ship was carrying a heavy load of cargo.

It was midnight. I prepared to bunk down for the night. By now I had learned through necessity how to sleep even in a bucket seat. I put my woolen scarf along one edge for a pillow. The ridge between the metal seats I fitted in about my belt line, twisted my legs into a sort of contorted S, and prepared to sleep. The ensign looked at me with what seemed great annoyance.

"Are you going to sleep tonight?" he demanded.

"Why not?" I asked.

"Haven't you heard of the trouble we've been having lately off the Bay of Biscay?"

"There's nothing *I* can do about it," I told him. "If we

are going to be shot down, I'd rather be asleep and know nothing about it."

I would not have slept so soundly had I known what he told me the next morning as we landed at Casablanca. Nazi planes had been flying out from bases somewhere along the coast of France or possibly Spain. But the night before our flight a C-54, identical with ours, had been shot down by British Spitfires when the American ship had flown unwittingly over a British convoy. It appeared there had been some confusion regarding identification. The Spitfires, flying sharply upward through a heavy overcast, had come upon the C-54 and, believing it to be a German raider, had opened fire.

Thus did I set foot upon the soil of Africa for the first time. Magnificent sunshine, a superabundance of oranges, eggs with shells on, and white bread—none of which I had seen for months in England—made Casablanca even more attractive. It had become, the war having passed over it, a giant air transport center. All day long, the loud-speaker commanded the attention of travelers to Dakar, to Algiers, to Cairo, to England, to the United States, and to virtually every other part of the globe except Nazi-held Europe.

It was good to sit in the sunshine in the lovely Place Lyautey, near the statue of the famous general and colonial administrator after whom the park had been named. It was pleasant of an evening to sit over a drink in the impressive Allied officers' club. Downstairs life imitated art in Rick's Café, patterned after the fictitious café of that name in the Humphrey Bogart picture, *Casablanca*. But it was open only to uniformed personnel. No woman was allowed to enter unless she were Wac, Army nurse, or Red Cross worker. Hassocks were used instead of tables. Sometimes we were amused to see a healthy American woman from Iowa or

Mississippi getting a vicarious thrill under the dim lights as she sat with a uniformed companion and tried to make herself believe that he looked like Bogart. But one soon learned that, though the war had come and gone in Casablanca, its surface beauty masked intrigue, corruption, poverty, and ignorance. I looked in vain for schools for the huge Arab population. French men and women who had fled to North Africa when France fell, carrying with them as much of their wealth as they could manage, plotted and intrigued as they almost literally stood poised like birds of prey to fly back to France to resume the old way of life as soon as the Nazis were ousted.

When the Germans controlled the north coast of Africa, many of the motley crew of Vichy French, German "tourists," and the dregs of adventurers from all over the face of the earth had collaborated gladly and profitably with the Germans. Now that the Allies were in control, the same crew fastened upon the Americans, alleging that they had always been stalwart fighters for the democratic process. One night in the lobby of the Excelsior Hotel, in which ATC fliers and other American Army personnel were billeted, one of these adventurers who had the temerity to invade a building controlled by the United States Army was pointed out. We were told he was an international spy, profitably in the pay of three groups, each violently antagonistic to the others. One of them was American.

Many of the groups in Casablanca at that time made no attempt to conceal strong pro-Nazi sympathy. The black market was incredible. One day Carleton Kent of the Chicago *Times* was approached on the street and offered four and one half times the price he had paid for the trench coat he was wearing. The offer was raised again and again when he refused to sell until it reached six times the original cost before he was finally able to shake off the importunities of the would-be purchaser. We found out afterward that trench coats like Kent's were selling for as high as eight times their cost. Sugar sold for a dollar a pound; butter, fifteen dollars for a five-pound can; a bar of laundry soap cost from a dollar and seventy cents or two-fifty, if delivered. We paid four cents for the same bar of soap in the American Army post exchange. Bed sheets brought ten dollars each. Cigarettes of the cheapest sort were fifty to sixty cents a package. Even at these prices there were few goods to be had.

I was shocked at the treatment of the Arabs who had burst into revolt at Fez and Rabat a few weeks before. French troops had suppressed the outbreak with some loss of life. There were three classes of ration books—one for white gentiles, one for Jews, and a third for Arabs. The cards permitted purchases on a descending scale in the order named.

This differentiation on the basis of color was an innovation which arrived with the Americans and British. Since before the days of the Saracens, North Africa has been a melting pot in which the blood of all races has mingled. But now attempts were being made to teach the natives that skin color made a difference in human relations. In Casablanca, Algiers, Tunis, and other North African cities segregation had been established. An Army chaplain told me, "There have been numerous instances where American prejudice has tried, and in some instances has succeeded, right here in this theater, to show itself in dealing with Negro troops. For instance, the French and Spanish people have been told that the Negro troops are not clean or healthy; that they are beastly and inhuman and should not be associated with. When the natives here refused to listen to such tommyrot and continued to associate with the Negro troops, all who were found walking the streets with Negro troops were immediately arrested by the French police, at the instigation of the American Army authorities, and taken to headquarters for examination for disease. In this manner they have intimidated the girls of this area so that now you hardly ever see one walking with a colored soldier in the city."

An interesting story developed in the establishment of Red Cross clubs at Casablanca soon after Allied troops had landed there. Following the usual Red Cross pattern, one club was for the use of white soldiers, the other for the use of Negroes. The Negro club's director was energetic and affable Sidney Williams, formerly secretary of the National Urban League at Cleveland, Ohio. Mr. Williams was able to get kitchen and snack-bar equipment for his club some weeks before the "white" club could get theirs. Because the food was good and the atmosphere friendly and congenial, American soldiers, white and colored, flocked to the "Negro" Red Cross club, somewhat to the embarrassment of those who insisted on the pattern of American segregation even in Africa.

Good fortune attended me at Casablanca. Because of a difference of opinion between military authorities and war correspondents which had occurred prior to my arrival in North Africa, accreditation of virtually all war correspondents had been stopped. I had been accredited only to Casablanca and from there to French West Africa, French Equatorial Africa, and other countries. When I walked into the Public Relations Office at Casablanca and introduced myself, a captain, slight of build and studious of appearance, greeted me warmly. He told me that on several occasions he and I had almost been introduced to each other in New

York, and here we were meeting nearly four thousand miles away from the city in which we had lived but a few blocks from each other. Considerably past the draft age, Martin Kamin hated Nazis with such a burning hatred he had almost literally fought his way into the Army. Master of seven languages, omnivorous reader and student of history, he was then engaged in handling Army Public Relations and in writing for the Army a history of sections of the North African campaign against Rommel. No war correspondent ever talked with Captain Kamin without learning not only movements of troops and tactics of battle but equally the forces of human ideas and acts which motivate military campaigns.

Because the headquarters of the North African Theater of Operations was now at Algiers, Captain Kamin suggested that I proceed there to clear up the matter of accreditation. When I reported to theater headquarters in Algiers, Major General David Barr, theater chief of staff, who had been most helpful to me in London, asked if I had stopped at Oran on my way from Casablanca. He declined to tell me why I should have done so or why he thought I should return there immediately instead of stopping off after I had been further east.

I left early the next morning in General Barr's plane. Little did I dream when, on the way from Casablanca, the plane stopped at Oran for a very poor luncheon at the airport that so vast and efficient an Army installation had been built up at Oran. The largest military hospital outside of the United States, and possibly the largest in the world, had been built almost literally overnight there on the shores of the Mediterranean. If there was any facility lacking for the treatment of any physical, mental, or other need, my inexpert eye failed to notice it. The wards were dotted here and there with Negro casualties. One of them, a sergeant from a small Louisiana town, had had most of his right thigh shot away as he and other quartermaster troops landed supplies at the Anzio beachhead. He told us that he had begun to believe that his was a charmed life since he had also made the beachhead landings at Sicily and Salerno.

I was reminded again of the contradictions of race in the Army. The theory seemed to be that men, when fighting or preparing to fight, had to be kept racially apart. But I had found two phases of Army life where segregation was neither practiced nor apparently believed necessary—in conscientious objectors' camps and in hospitals. In England I had seen this in numerous Army hospitals—one of them an excellently run and superbly equipped institution whose large staff of doctors, nurses, and technicians was made up, with but one or two exceptions, of Texans. But in that hospital, and all others I visited, soldiers were assigned to wards and buildings on the basis of their maladies and not according to skin color.

A tremendous replacement depot through which passed daily thousands of men either being evacuated from Italy or en route to the Italian front, the Middle East, the Burma-China or other theaters gave it the appearance of an outdoor Grand Central Terminal. Three thousand men could be fed every hour. Because of the scarcity of wood and other fuel, gasoline was used temporarily to cook the food.

A quiet Texan, Colonel Charles W. Christianberry, whose manner was more that of a college professor than a warrior, directed the depot. When I noticed in one of the mess halls white and colored officers eating together, I mentioned the fact to Colonel Christianberry. He smiled, saying, "We are all fighting the same war together, aren't we?" When I remarked that it was interesting to hear a

Texan express such an attitude, he told me how it had developed. He had attended Columbia University and had been professor of military science at New York University for eight years. But his conviction that all human beings should be treated alike regardless of race had developed before he left Fort Worth. Colonel Christianberry was a devout Christian. He had arrived in his own thinking at the conclusion that, if all men are brothers, they should be treated as brothers. When one of his subordinate officers had urged racial segregation at Oran because there had been instances of friction, the colonel had asked him who the aggressors were. The officer had replied that they were white soldiers.

"And you propose that we segregate and penalize those who were imposed upon instead of those who did the imposing?"

There had been no further complaints, Colonel Christianberry told me, or demands that segregation be established.

Unhappily, the same courage and vision had not been exhibited by the Red Cross. Two segregated clubs for Negroes had been established; one of them, called the "Country Club," had an exceedingly attractive recreation hall built of native stone and wood from packing cases by Italian prisoners of war. It was in the auditorium of this building that the glee club of the 484th Engineers Battalion sang for me. But as I watched their faces I became painfully conscious that the Negro of World War II was not a laughing Negro. The "sense of humor" which the Octavus Roy Cohens and the Irvin Cobbs invariably attribute to the Negro has been replaced by the warrior. One felt it in that auditorium on the shores of the Mediterranean as the chorus sang "Show Me the Way" and "God Shall Wipe All Tears Away."

At Oran, where a Negro unit had a difficult and responsible assignment, it was discharged with pride in contrast to the attitude toward the menial tasks in labor groups. I wondered at the blindness of America in crushing or by indifference permitting to be crushed the eagerness of its Negro citizens to participate fully and to contribute generously to the building of a strong America.

And then I was taken to a hillside from whose natural amphitheater one looked out upon the blue expanse of the Mediterranean. At the foot of the hill was a microphone to which I was escorted. Seated on the hillside were between five and six thousand Negro soldiers. The late afternoon sun lighted up the thousands of battle helmets. An ominous, brooding, intent silence hung like a pall over them. Little applause, even of the courtesy variety, followed my introduction. The unit had been trained in the United States for combat and shipped overseas a few weeks before I encountered them at Oran. But they had arrived in North Africa at a time when port battalions were needed to unload ships. Though there were many Italian prisoners of war available for such manual labor, and a large number of American soldiers who had been inactive at Oran for some time who might have served as port battalions, the decision had been made instead to transform this outfit from combat to service status. Having steeled themselves to combat and having eagerly anticipated service as fighting men, the sudden transition had driven morale to the vanishing point. A few attempted to rationalize what had happened to them by saying that as service troops they would be less likely to get killed. But that comfort, such as it was, was short-lived. In modern warfare the order in beachhead landings is, first, assault troops; second, engineers to rebuild bridges and repair roads and clear away debris; third, quartermaster troops bringing food, medical supplies, and ammunition. An army always attacks the supply lines of the enemy. Men handling bulldozers, driving trucks, handling supplies, are unable simultaneously to do those things and man guns. Thus these men knew that, in addition to the humiliation of being reduced from fighting men to manual laborers, the hazard of life was increased.

No speech I have ever made before or since was more difficult than the feeble and ineffective one on that occasion. I could only assure them that I knew the reasons for their dejection and that those of us who were in a position to would do all we could.

Chapter Eight

---❖---

IN THE SPRING of 1944 it was difficult to believe that Algiers had been so recently the center of desperate warfare or that a few weeks later, at the time of the invasion of southern France, it would again move into the headlines of battle. This was true even though one saw everywhere on its wind-swept streets the uniforms of the French, British, American, Polish, Senegalese, and other armies. Occasionally we went through air-raid alerts; more occasionally, air raids.

In the Aletti Hotel, which had been taken over for the accommodation of American and British officers, there was an almost drowsy atmosphere. Attractive French and Algerian girls wearing wooden-soled shoes, which made a terrific clatter on the tiled floor of the dining room, served colonels, majors, brigadier generals, and a constantly changing flood of civilian officials guarding closely bulging attaché cases.

Seven rooms, each with two beds, were reserved at the Aletti for war correspondents. One never knew who would share his room with him on any given night. One night I retired around nine o'clock as I was to leave very early the next morning for Italy. On being awakened, I found that Eric Sevareid was asleep in the other bed. I tiptoed about so as not to awaken him and we did not speak. Perhaps some-day we will meet when both of us are awake.

But the outward calm of Algiers was illusory. It was then the headquarters of De Gaulle and the French Committee of National Liberation. Various pressures were being brought to bear on the Committee. The French underground was insisting that the Committee repudiate by action as well as deed all those who collaborated with Vichy in any fashion. In a little café near the water-front building in which the as-sembly of the FCNL gathered one could meet, if he were properly vouched for, emaciated, haggard French men and women who had miraculously escaped from France as emis-saries of the resistance movement. It was startling to learn how much traffic was going on between North Africa and Vichy. Some of the stories of the dangers encountered and escaped from by the messengers of the underground were sometimes so melodramatic as to be almost incredible. And then there was the easier travel back and forth, aided by the Gestapo and by some of the pro-Nazis who were still operating in North Africa, of those who still did business with Vichy and Berlin.

There were also the various pressures upon the FCNL by England, Russia, and United States. It was generally be-lieved that some of the trials and executions of collabora-tors during the winter and spring of 1944 were designed to give assurance to the underground and Russia that the FCNL did not intend to play ball with any Frenchmen who had trafficked with the enemies of France.

Because there was little to do of an evening in Algiers, the war correspondents, after dinner, would frequently gather in one of the seven rooms for conversation. There was Harold Callender of the New York *Times;* Sonia Tomara of the New York *Herald Tribune;* Bill Shenkel, who not long afterward was shot down and killed in the first B-29 raid on Japan; handsome Max Hill of NBC, who looks like a younger edition of Hemingway; and other British and American correspondents who formed this group. Almost from day to day the personnel changed. A war correspondent would suddenly descend upon us from India or Burma and make "Vinegar Joe" Stilwell's desperate fight for the Ledo Road no farther away than Naples. A night or two later another would arrive from Washington or New York to tell us of the latest outburst in Congress by a politician more concerned with his re-election than with the war. A very quiet correspondent of a South African paper calmly dismissed as routine and unimportant his having crash-landed deep in the interior of Africa and traveled afoot and by the most primitive means to get to a town. From his tone one would have imagined the incident no more important than the difficulty of getting a taxicab in New York City. But the hazards of warfare and travel were calmly accepted as being part of the job.

General Pucheu was then on trial in Algiers for his life, charged with having surrendered too willingly to the Germans in Tunisia. It was a weird spectacle. Prosecution and defense introduced little evidence. The occasion was one for oratory as a means of telling the world each side's version of what would happen in the future more than what had happened in the past. On the terrace of the Aletti I received from the correspondents covering the trial an invaluable education as to what really had motivated the spectacle and what probably lay ahead. Later, after I had returned to America, I read some of the versions and interpretations of the trial which had been cabled to the United States. Except for some of those written by war correspondents, it was difficult for me to believe they dealt with the trial which I had attended. Some of them were written as though there had been neither revolution nor war nor other change in the world; where the war was recognized as existing, the impression was given that it was but a temporary dislocation after which the world would resume its former state without change of rulers and ruled.

In January there had been held at Brazzaville, French Equatorial Africa, under the auspices of the FCNL, a conference of the governors and administrators of the French colonies in Africa. A revised colonial policy had been presented for discussion which included extension of education and health services and economic opportunity for natives. Mlle. Eve Curie, now a lieutenant in the French Army; René Pleven, Minister of Colonies; André Laguerre, of the Ministry of Information; and other officials of the De Gaulle government supplied interesting information and side lights on what the colonial policy of France, when and if restored, would be. It was clear that she did not intend to give up her colonial possessions nor the wealth or man power derived from the colonies. It was also apparent that France knew and recognized more clearly than other colonial powers that she could not hope to retain control nor command the loyalty of French colonials unless the demands for greater participation of the colonies and of the administration itself were at least partially met. So, too, was France recognizing that the growing Pan-Arabic movement had to be recognized and at least some of its demands met or there would be continued and growing revolt. White nations and peoples had vigorously proclaimed to the world that this war is being fought for freedom, and colored peoples were taking them at face value.

I thought again of Wendell Willkie's statement in *One World:*

I know that the retention of points such as Suez, the eastern Mediterranean and the routes through Asia Minor to the east, obviously, if our western democracy is not to be threatened by hostile forces, must be kept in both friendly and stabilized hands. Likewise, I know there is much historical and even present day justification for the current "protective" colonial system. Pragmatically, however, in view of the ferment which is going on, it is a question whether that system can be maintained. Idealistically, we must face the fact that the system is completely antipathetic to all the principles for which we claim to fight. Furthermore, the more we approach those principles, the more we stimulate the ferment that endangers the system.

I thought of this quotation as I sought unsuccessfully to get exact information on the Arab revolts that had taken place early in the year at Fez, Rabat, and Marrakech. I was told that Nazi propaganda was responsible for the outbreaks. I asked about the leaflets in Arabic reading "Down with Hitler, Down with De Gaulle. Long Live Roosevelt and the Atlantic Charter," that had been distributed. I could get no satisfactory explanation when I remarked that I did not believe that the Nazis would be subtle or courageous enough to include "Down with Hitler" in any of their propaganda.

Harried by the uncertainty of the attitude toward France, and particularly toward the FCNL, of England and the United States, understandably suspicious of England's attitude and action in what had formerly been French territory and particularly in the Middle East where the recent Lebanese riots had occurred, De Gaulle and his fellow members of the FCNL were desperate and unhappy. Less addicted to color prejudice than England and America, the French were unhappy about concessions regarding her colored colonies which the FCNL apparently felt were necessary until the future of France had been determined. One note was encouraging, however—that the Brazzaville Conference at least indicated that the France which was struggling to rise to her feet again was aware that the whole colonial system would have to be patched up and modified.

Chapter Nine

———————◆———————

WE WERE SCHEDULED to leave the Maison Blanche Airport at Algiers early Sunday morning in a giant DC-3, flown by a British crew. The center of the plane, lengthwise, was piled high with the luggage of the British PRO which, following the progress then being made by the Allied armies in Italy, was shifting its headquarters from Algiers to Naples. Bundled in Mae West belts and once again briefed in the use of life rafts, because German planes were still active in the region, we were ready to take off when one of the engines failed. We were allowed to leave the plane but not the field. When we returned to the plane, the other American aboard, a captain of the Army Pictorial Services, and I found all the seats pre-empted except two up in front which, in the very bumpy weather over Sicily, became even more uncomfortable than bucket seats usually are.

We were scheduled to land at Capodichino Airport at Naples, but a low ceiling necessitated our landing instead at the Pomigliano Airport, which had been virtually destroyed. It was the first area I had seen where the destruction had been done by our planes instead of by those of the enemy. My respect for American Liberators as implements of destruction matched that of the Italians. For many blocks in every direction from Pomigliano buildings had been leveled to rubble. But one section of one of the airport buildings remained standing and was now being used as operational headquarters for the field when emergency landings had to be made there. The parts of the walls which remained standing were cracked in many places. Only a few panes of glass remained in a two-story-high window over a stairway. The window bellied inward and seemed about to collapse at the slightest provocation.

The APS captain had been charged, just as we left Algiers, with the responsibility of delivering eleven precious sacks of mail. He could not leave the Naples airport until someone in authority arrived to take possession of the bags. So disorganized were all services, including the telephone, in Naples at the time that it was two hours before a truck arrived to transport the mail and ourselves into Naples. We sat on the side of an open truck in a driving rainstorm, the water sloshing about our ankles as we drove into Naples. Hardly one building stood intact and unbombed. It was like a deserted village except for the miserably clad, emaciated Italians, either very old or very young. Once again the sheer wastefulness of war hung like a pall over the scene.

Correspondents were housed in a beautiful villa high above Naples, overlooking the harbor and Vesuvius. Despite the cold, driving rain, it was beautiful. But there was neither heat nor hot water nor blankets. The cold, damp air seemed to be imbedded in the beautiful tiled floors and to press in upon one from the walls and ceiling like the freezing of a barrel of cider in the wintertime, ourselves imprisoned in the center.

But our living quarters were luxurious compared to those of the people of Naples. Fantastically ornate buildings erected by Mussolini in the vicinity of Villa Roma and Villa San Felice, some of which had been used for Fascist headquarters or for other purposes to give the illusion of progress and prosperity, provided a bitterly ironic commentary on the Fascist economy. American Army trucks and jeeps were to be seen everywhere in the refuse-filled streets. But they seemed no more numerous than the ornate hearses one could not escape in any part of Naples. Typhus, starvation, venereal disease, and other maladies were taking a terrible toll of people weakened to the point of exhaustion by the ravages of war. What Allied bombers had left untouched the Germans had destroyed with land mines and time bombs before evacuating the city. Virtually no bridges were left standing. Every few miles railroad tracks formed grotesque figures like the curved front runners on sleighs, as the result of land mines.

At the time the Germans had stopped the Allies cold at Cassino. At Anzio, the triangular beachhead, then about eight miles from Anzio to Nettuno and running a dozen miles inland, threatened to become another Dunkirk as the Allied soldiers desperately fought back the waves of German infantry, air, and artillery attacks. So grim and perilous a picture did Naples present as the focal point of Allied attack at that time, one felt convinced that the traditional saying, "See Naples and die," should be rewritten to "See Naples die."

But the morale of Negro soldiers in the Italian Theater was higher than in any other theater of operation I had visited. The reasons were simple. There was, first, the presence of Negro combat troops as well as service battalions. The 99th Pursuit Squadron was then coming into its own and beginning to receive the recognition its feats merited. At the beginning of the war Negroes had been told bluntly that they would not be admitted to the Air Corps. That publicized and glamorized branch of the armed services was to be kept lily-white. Enormous pressure, climaxed by the resignation in protest of Judge William H. Hastie as civilian aide to the Secretary of War, had been necessary to achieve even slight modification of the ban. Even then it had been modified only to the extent of permitting Negroes to be trained at a segregated school at Tuskegee Institute, Alabama. The sole training given them was as pursuit fliers, generally regarded as the most hazardous of all flying.

Even after completing the course the 99th had encountered skepticism on all sides as to the ability of Negroes as aviators. On being sent overseas to North Africa, the 99th had been made one of the four squadrons of the 79th Pursuit Group. Some 40 per cent of the personnel of the other three squadrons were fliers from the South. But when, as the famous "Falcon Desert Fighter Group," as the 79th became known, they participated in the bitterly fought North African campaign, all four squadrons found themselves and were forged by necessity and experience into one of the most effective fighting units of the United States Army. Flying P-40s, low-altitude ships, the group, and particularly the 99th, became adept in skillful, reckless dive-bombing of enemy targets. Whatever prejudice, created by race and environment, existed on either side when the group was activated began to seem a bit superfluous and even silly in the face of death and danger. The experience gained in North Africa, Sicily, and now in Italy had earned them the reputation of being the "hottest fighting unit in Italy."

One morning we stood in the operations building of the Capodichino Airport. A huge map covered one side of the square, flat-topped, boxlike building. A Negro sergeant was marking on the map the bomb runs for the mission about to start, not only for the 99th but for the other squadrons of the 79th Group. Across the way, a second Negro sergeant and a white one worked with heads close together on another technical preparation for the flight. Inside and outside, in the cold sunlight stood little groups of fighter pilots smoking a last cigarette together before climbing into their ships. A blind man could not have picked out the white or the Negro pilots. Democracy seemed more nearly achieved in that moment than it had ever seemed before, though it is tragic that a war of such proportions and destructiveness had apparently been necessary to cause Americans in isolated instances like this one to forego race prejudice. It was achieved much more easily by the 79th a day or two later. A dinner party had been arranged to celebrate the first anniversary of the 79th's entrance into combat with the enemy. The luxurious Allied officers' club, built high in the hills overlooking the Bay of Naples, was selected for the celebration. As far as I could learn, there had been no question nor thought of any arrangement except participation by every pilot of each of the four squadrons. But the arrangements committee found itself faced with an order prohibiting whites and Negroes from associating in any place where there was dancing. The reaction of the men was spontaneous and unanimous. "We've fought together, faced death together, and some of us have died together," was their reaction. "When we celebrate, we are going to celebrate together." The party was a success. No one seems to have been injured by fraternization.

General Mark Clark had requested the 99th to supply fighter escort for himself for a flight to the Anzio beachhead. Without bitterness or envy, some of the white fliers were congratulating and kidding members of the 99th on this tribute to their effectiveness. The 99th had flown up to that time, in Italy, a total of 450 missions and 2316 sorties. A number of the 99th had been killed in action or taken prisoner. Other Air Corps units had made as brilliant records, and some had made even more notable ones. But it was beginning to be recognized that none had been made in the face of greater difficulties than the 99th's.

The 99th had been recently joined in Italy by three other Negro squadrons—all flying P-39s. Arrangements were then being made to shift all four squadrons to the longer-range, heavier, and higher-altitude P-47s in anticipation of the invasion of Europe. Despite the remarkable success of the integration of the 99th Pursuit Squadron into the 79th Pursuit Group, it was then planned to establish an all-Negro pursuit group under the command of Lieutenant Colonel Benjamin O. Davis, Jr., by uniting the 99th with the other three squadrons. There were many of us who felt such a step would be a mistake. A successful establishment of the fact that Negro and white fliers could bridge the chasm created by race should be continued. It was proposed to the War Department that the 99th continue as a part of the 79th and that another fighter squadron be combined with the other three squadrons to provide a second "mixed unit," this one under the leadership of Colonel Davis, who is a West Point graduate and a brilliant Negro officer. As I write, the first of these recommendations has been adopted by the War Department. All the squadrons continue to make brilliant records despite heavy casualties in the invasion from the south of Europe.

Another courageous and even more hazardous, though less publicized, accomplishment by Negro troops in Italy at that time further bolstered morale of Negro troops. The position of Allied troops on the Anzio beachhead was one of great peril at that time. Hitler was determined to prevent the capture of Rome. He threw into the task of stopping the Allied troops many of his most experienced divisions.

Day and night assaults were made upon the beleaguered Allies hemmed in the Anzio triangle. Three huge guns, mounted on railway carriages nicknamed by the Americans "Whistling Willies," shuttled in and out of tunnels just north of the beachhead to lay down a barrage of 340-millimeter shells on the eight-mile strip of beach whenever LSTs attempted to land desperately needed supplies of ammunition, medicine, food, and troops. The LSTs were loaded at Naples. All crew members, correspondents, and troops were required to get aboard at noon. The LSTs sailed about dusk, straight out to sea westward, turned due north and out of range of Nazi planes. Opposite the beachhead they turned sharply eastward, timed to reach the beachhead in the dim light of dawn to unload the trucks and other vehicles, take aboard the vehicles and wounded to be returned to Naples, and depart before they could be dive-bombed or shelled.

Frequently—as a matter of fact, more often than otherwise—the approach of the LSTs to shore was the signal for a terrific barrage of German shells which literally laid down a curtain of fire. Though the Allies held air superiority over the beachhead, suicide squadrons of Nazi dive bombers frequently broke through in desperate efforts to drop bombs upon the ships. Until the curtain of fire was slackened, the slow-moving and vulnerable ships were forced to remain stationary in the harbor, targets of concentrated bombardment.

Some 70 per cent of the quartermaster and port battalion troops operating these LSTs were Negroes. The very heavy loss of life was inevitable. Of a single battalion of Negro troops, 52 were killed and 93 injured within a few days at the beachhead. But, according to Colonel Whitman, of Connecticut, the C.O. of the men running supplies to Anzio, he had great difficulty in persuading men under his command, who had returned from the beachhead in the morning, from going out again in the afternoon. When I later asked at Naples to see photographs which the United States Army had taken of the dramatic scenes at Anzio, I was told that none had been taken.

One of the most important of all lessons a war correspondent must learn is to avoid losing one's way near battle fronts. Ollie Harrington of the Pittsburgh *Courier*, Art Carter of the Baltimore *Afro-American*, Lieutenant James Freeman of the 99th Pursuit Squadron, and I were taught this lesson at the Cassino front in Italy.

The four of us set out from Naples early in the morning for Cassino. The Army Public Relations Office had instructed us to go to a certain place from which Colonel Kenneth Clark would give us further directions. Through bomb- and shell-battered Capua, made famous by Shakespeare, and through equally battered Caserta we drove over roads which became more and more choked with vehicles and men moving up to the front. The heavy, high-bodied reconnaissance car which can go almost anywhere a jeep can bumped its way over recently shelled roads which had been hastily and expertly repaired. A friendly Military Police officer in a markedly Southern accent offered us motorcycle escort to Colonel Clark's tent which we gladly accepted.

Colonel Clark turned out to be an old friend I had met some years ago when he was a New York newspaperman. He told us to avoid Route 6 as Nazi guns were blazing at it and to take a somewhat more circuitous road to the front line, where we could find the New Zealand headquarters from which the battle was being directed. There we would be given a guide to take us to the crest of a hill which was the nearest point to Cassino to which it was safe for correspondents to go. But even as he was telling us this, Bill Morgan of the Chicago *Daily News*, with whom I had been billeted at Algiers and Naples, entered the tent to inform us that he and other correspondents had just been shelled by the Germans at the hill. The four of us decided not to let this discourage us so we set out, along roads even more choked, for the place where the New Zealand command was located. The sound of guns and exploding shells grew louder and louder. Ammunition trucks filled to the brim moved up to the line of battle; ambulances almost as full of wounded moved back from the line.

We had not noticed a 155-millimeter gun emplaced by the road as we drove toward it. We did notice it, however, when it was fired as we drove past it. Back in Naples our car had seemed heavy and solid. But now the tremendous concussion of the huge gun lifted it up and over to the right as Lieutenant Freeman skillfully wrenched the wheel to the left to avoid capsizing.

It was about that time that Freeman began to wonder if we should not have arrived at the New Zealand command's station. But Carter confidently assured him it was a mile and a half farther on. As he had been there before, we continued to drive. Suddenly a New Zealand sentry rushed in front of our car, commanding us to stop. Shouting to make myself heard over the roar of the guns, I asked him where we could find his command. Pointing back down the road on which we had traveled with such difficulty, he informed us, "It is four and a half miles back!" I asked him where we were. He pointed to a pool of smoke and dust in the valley below us and answered, "*That* is Cassino!"

On our way back from Cassino we drove somewhat parallel to the battle front toward Venafro. As we reached the crest of the hill looking out over a landscape where every house had been destroyed by the terrific bombardment, we met several truckloads of Negro engineers headed toward the front. From them we learned the tragic story which illustrated that infallibility of airmen was not a characteristic of race, creed, or nationality. A squadron of American bombers had mistaken Venafro for their target, which was Cassino. Several hundred French and American soldiers had been killed or injured.

My companions and I were deeply touched by the expressions on the faces of the Negro soldiers on encountering Negro war correspondents. I presented Ollie Harrington and Art Carter as war correspondents of two of the largest American Negro newspapers, and Jim as an officer of the famous 99th. The faces of the men were wreathed in pleasant smiles of satisfaction. An amusing episode occurred when Ollie introduced me. The men were standing close-packed in the trucks. One of them leaned over in astonishment and asked if it were really true that I was the Walter White who was the secretary of the NAACP. When I assured him I was, he exclaimed, "What the hell are you doing up here where all the shooting is going on?" When I countered by reminding him that he, too, was there, he answered, "I gotta be here because the draft board said so, but you don't have to!"

But beneath the banter was a tremendous happiness among the men that war correspondents of their own race were also in the war zones, reporting the grim story as it unfolded.

We were at Cassino when the going was toughest for the Allies. We had asked to be directed to the sections of the battle front where American troops were stationed. The soldiers who were taking the tremendous pounding of German mortars sheltered in tunnels and in caves at the crest of Mount Cassino and the abbey were largely New Zealanders, Indians, and Pasutos from Africa. Some of these Allied troops had been completely isolated in the hills around Cassino to such an extent that ammunition, goods, and medical supplies had to be dropped down to them by parachute. Later, when the pressure by American airmen and ground troops finally wore down the Germans, the American and British troops were returned to the line to make the triumphal entry into Cassino and through it to Rome.

None of the American, British, or other war correspondents were conscious of any deliberate intent to ignore the accomplishments of colored troops. In the first place, confinement of Negroes, particularly in the American Army, to service units, where their work was of non-spectacular character, militated against their sharing in the glamorous and news-making phases of the war. This contributed to correspondents understandably devoting their attention to the deeds of the more dramatic branches of the service. White quartermaster and engineer units suffer from the same disadvantages as do the Negro quartermaster and engineer corps. Ollie Harrington talked one day at Anzio with Ernie Pyle, who quite frankly admitted that until Ollie called his attention to the part Negro soldiers were playing it had not occurred to him to look for material among Negro units. In his widely syndicated column Pyle subsequently began to call attention to the role which Negro soldiers play.

Such incidents as these are not frequent. A Negro trucking company was being settled for the night at Bagnoli, near the Italian front. German fighters suddenly appeared overhead, dropping flares, followed by German dive bombers and heavy bombers. Having just arrived in the area, there were no foxholes or slit trenches in which the men could take refuge. The Negro sergeant, from a little town in southern New Jersey, told me the story of how the men dispersed to seek shelter. He ducked under a weapons carrier. Down swept the German planes, loosing racks of bombs. One bomb dropped thirty yards away from the sergeant; a second twenty yards away. A white-hot piece of shrapnel went through the heavy, solid rubber tire and floor of the weapons carrier. A private from Louisiana who had taken shelter with the sergeant was mortally wounded. The sergeant crawled over to him to give him aid. He found that the whole of the private's back had been blown away and that he was beyond help.

At that moment fire broke out when one of the German flares landed on top of a tent, making the whole area a target for the bombers sweeping down from overhead. Near by was a motor pool of valuable vehicles loaded with supplies. The sergeant crawled out from under the weapons carrier and ran across the brightly lighted area to secure fire extinguishers from the trucks. The sergeant's lieutenant and captain emerged from their place of refuge, bringing water to aid in putting out the flames of the burning tent. But before the fire could be put out German planes returned to strafe. Back under the weapons carrier went the sergeant, and elsewhere went the lieutenant and the captain. The fire broke out again. His superior officers did not return. The water was gone and fire extinguishers were empty. The sergeant dug dirt with his battle helmet and a shovel from one of the trucks and threw the dirt on the fire; again and again he did this, but before he could put it out the strafing planes returned. When they had finally passed, he emerged once more and this time succeeded in extinguishing the flames. Of eighty-five drivers of the trucks in the motor pool, thirteen were killed and ten injured. The sergeant summoned the medical detachment and aided them in locating the injured by the sounds of their groans in the darkness. The sergeant was cited for his courage and awarded the silver star. But the news was published only in the Negro papers.

Another Negro soldier, a private from Pittsburgh, Pennsylvania, in a quartermaster trucking company, evacuated, while continuously under shellfire for more than three hours, twelve hundred wounded white soldiers near Cassino. When the road became unusable because of continuous enemy shellfire, this Negro private used stone and dirt to make negotiable the bed of a dry stream to get the wounded to safety.

A Negro automatic weapons company was twice cited by General Mark Clark for shooting down Nazi planes between Naples and Venafro. A Negro private from Detroit was awarded the silver star for capturing, singlehanded, a German patrol of five soldiers.

But these and other examples of heroism are often lost in the more dramatic and more publicized achievements of white soldiers.

Chapter Ten

————◆————

SOME VERY INTERESTING contrasts in the prevalence and virulence of racial prejudice in theaters of active war and theaters of preparation for action were found in Italy. On the Villa San Felice stands a flamboyantly colorful building erected by the Fascists. It was now an enlisted men's Red Cross club through which poured a steady stream of GIs of every race, creed, color, and national origin. As far as could be learned, this arrangement was satisfactory and there had been no instances of friction between soldiers of different racial background. But Naples was then becoming increasingly crowded with American soldiers for the drive on Rome. Among these were many Negro troops, chiefly of service divisions. The Red Cross thereupon opened a Jim Crow club in a somewhat dilapidated building on a back street. One of the reasons given was the old chestnut, "Negroes will be happier in a club of their own."

A few American white soldiers assiduously sought to spread anti-Negro propaganda among the Italians. A cheaply printed handbill, purporting to be a Neapolitan street song, mysteriously appeared in quantities in Naples. It bore the title " *'E femmene Italiana sotto 'e brace de Negre e a Americane* [Italian Women Arm in Arm with American Negroes]." It was to be sung to the tune of a Neapolitan song whose English title is "A Cup of Coffee." The verses vilified Italian women who associated with Negroes, declaring that it was only to rob colored soldiers of their money and threatening dire revenge upon these women when their husbands, "now prisoners of war," returned home.

Investigation by General David G. Barr, chief of staff of the Mediterranean Theater of Operations, resulted in the apprehension of the Italians responsible for the printing and distribution of these pamphlets. The investigation assumed that the purpose was to capitalize financially on presumed prejudice of white Americans against Negro Americans. Some doubt, however, is cast upon this motive as the leaflets were printed in Italian, with which language few of the American soldiers were familiar. Inasmuch as the leaflets were very cheaply printed and given away, it seemed reasonable to assume that there was other motivation behind the printing and distribution by Italians than that of making a meager profit from such copies of the leaflet as might be sold.

An even more blatant appeal to prejudice was found in a well-printed placard, twenty-four by thirty-six inches, which appeared on billboards in Naples one morning. Also printed in Italian, this placard purported to be issued by the Italian-American Committee for the Preservation of the Italian Race. The placard melodramatically appealed to Italians to refrain from associating with American Negro troops. "Do you not know that the Negro is a man of the colored races; that he must live in America only among his own; that he is an inferior human being, if not in name, at least in fact?" the placard proclaimed. Physical violence was threatened against any Italian woman seen associating with American Negroes, such threats being used as "the machine gun will cut down the prostitute who sells the honor of her race, and the people will seek revenge upon her and her black son when this crime has been brought to light." General Barr also ordered an investigation of the distribution of this publication.

The investigation disclosed that no such organization as the Italian-American Committee for the Preservation of the Italian Race existed, nor could any person be found of the name "R. A. Jacono," which was signed on the placard as president of the Committee. According to General Barr, "The investigation revealed that an American soldier, of Italian extraction, was fully responsible for this poster. This soldier, and two others who had assisted in financing and distributing the poster, have subsequently been tried and convicted by court-martial under the 96th Article of War."

There are four reasons, however, why attempts to spread anti-Negro prejudice met with indifferent success in Italy. The first of these has already been mentioned—the salutary effect of the presence of Negro combat troops which, though few in number, created a reputation among both Americans and Italians that Negroes were fighting men as well as noncombat troops. The second deterrent was the alertness of some of the Army officials in investigating, apprehending, and punishing those responsible for the spreading of prejudice. A third reason was the blunt refusal of most of the Italians to believe stories that Negroes had tails, were illiterate, and were savage brutes. Too many of them had learned from firsthand acquaintance that among the Negro soldiers were men of culture and education. One morning a group of us were leaving the quarters of the 99th Pursuit Squadron on our way to the flying field. Outside the gates was the usual crowd of children begging for *caramelle*. One of the older children, a lad of ten or eleven, walked along with us. "Why do the white Americans say you are monkeys with tails?" he asked in honest puzzlement of the captain who shortly afterward was awarded the distinguished flying cross.

The fourth reason dealt with the object most dear to the hearts and stomachs of the Italians—food! Possibly in violation of Army regulations, mess sergeants, touched by the poverty and hunger of Italians, especially children, were in the habit of giving whatever food was left over from a meal to the Italians in the vicinity. Certainly in violation of Army regulations, there was considerable pilfering by some of the quartermaster troops, white as well as Negro. It appeared that the majority of the white culprits sold what they had stolen in the black market. In one instance in North Africa two deserters from the American Army and one from the French Army had secured a captain's, a first lieutenant's, and a sergeant's uniform. The sergeant's uniform was given to the Frenchman because he could speak the language. The trio appropriated an American Army staff car in which they would intercept a supply truck to whose driver the captain would declare that he commanded a highly secret installation near by whose supplies had failed to arrive. The captain would then order the driver of the supply truck to deposit his load just off the road. His men would pick up the food later.

For some time they were able to get away with their racket, selling the supplies at exorbitant prices to black-market operators. Eventually, however, they were apprehended and sentenced to long terms in prison. Negro quartermaster troops, however, more frequently pilfered, usually in smaller quantities, and gave the loot to starving Italians. Such generosity inevitably created an inordinate amount of good will for the Negro benefactors and for

Negroes generally among the recipients of their benefactions.

A story was told me by a Negro officer which brought home the extent of the hunger and misery of Italy in more heartbreaking fashion than could be found in any volume of statistics. He was staying at a small hotel in an Italian city on leave. Weary of washing his own clothes in his helmet, he sought a laundry, but was warned that his clothes might not be returned because the proprietor could pay him the original cost of the garments and sell them for many times the price in the black market. The officer asked the maid in the hotel to launder his clothes. When they were returned to him, he paid her two hundred and fifty lira, which he estimated was at least twice the laundry cost, because she had kept his room in excellent condition. He was a little surprised at her lack of enthusiasm for his generosity. He supplemented the payment by offering her two bars of laundry soap which he had bought at the post exchange for eight lira, or eight cents. Her protestations of gratitude were effusive. When he asked the maid why she should be so much more appreciative of two bars of laundry soap than she had been of two hundred and fifty lira, she answered, "Signor, what is money when prices are so high and there is nothing to buy?" Conversation revealed that a loaf of bread weighing a kilo, or slightly more than two pounds, cost a hundred and fifty lira, while she earned sixty lira for a twelve-hour day. Without martyrdom, but instead with a sense of good fortune, she told him that her only food the day before had been a single slice of bread.

Somewhat ashamed that he had just eaten a bountiful meal in the American Army mess which had cost him only twenty lira, the officer presented the maid with his week's rations of two chocolate bars, a package of Life Savers, a small package of cookies, and a can of tomato juice—the total cost of which had been thirty-eight cents. At first grateful and then coldly suspicious, she told him, "All right, I'm ready."

Puzzled, he asked her, "For what?" To which she replied, "You can have me now."

Embarrassed at her assumption that she was expected to make payment for value received, and not wishing to offend her, he told her he neither expected nor wished any recompense. Still suspicious, she left the room to return shortly afterward with her daughter, who assisted her in the hotel and was as ill clad, emaciated, and unattractive as the mother. "I understand," the old woman stated bitterly. "I am old and ugly. Here is my daughter."

The officer eventually succeeded, in a mixture of Italian and English, in convincing the mother that his gift had been without strings and that he wished no payment. The result was even more embarrassing. Looking sixty-five but probably no more than thirty-five years of age, the miserably clad, starved product of dictatorship showered tears and kisses upon the officer's hand as she sobbed, "No one has ever been so kind to me before."

Chapter Eleven

———◆———

"WHO HOLDS CHAD holds Africa," said General Mangin.

In the dark months which preceded and followed the fall of France in June 1940 his aphorism was expanded by the appalling success of the German conquests to "Who holds Africa holds the fate of the world." The decision as to who would hold Africa lay in the hands of a black man—Félix Eboué, then Governor of Chad, one of the five provinces comprising French Equatorial Africa, whose Governor-General Eboué was destined to become. The story of his decision to defy Vichy constitutes at least a footnote to history which needs recording before it is forgotten so that the world may know the debt it owes to Eboué.

Only a few weeks before his death in May 1944 it had been my privilege to spend two interesting and delightful days at Cairo with Governor-General Eboué. I found that he had not photographed well; his pictures gave him a heavy, almost sodden look. His eyes were deep set but sparkled to match his gay and ready wit. None of the few articles which have been written about him and none of those who knew him with whom I talked had prepared me for the gaiety he exhibited. All had pictured him as a serious-minded, almost tragic person. But responsibility which would have crushed a weaker man, the vitiating effects of equatorial heat and disease, anxiety over the fate of his people and of his own family, had not been able to destroy the strength and ebullience of his character.

A few weeks before I talked with Eboué, I had dined in London with General Sicé and Sir Hanns Vischer of the British Colonial Office. Few living men know Africa as well as do these two men. General Sicé is tall and slender, his hair now silvered by more than sixty years, almost half of which he has spent as head of the medical and welfare services of French Equatorial Africa. It is he who has done much to check the ravages of sleeping sickness and malaria, which have taken the lives of countless thousands in a region where the thermometer averages well over 100 degrees the year round. I had prepared a series of questions to ask General Sicé. Here is the composite answer he and others made which tells the story of Eboué's decision in 1940, upon which hung the fate not only of the black people of Africa but of white, brown, and yellow peoples throughout the world.

At no time in all human history has the outlook been more hopeless for successful resistance against armed might. During the preceding ten months Germany had invaded Poland, Denmark, Norway, the Netherlands, Belgium, and Luxembourg. The humiliating disaster of Dunkirk and the terrible bombing of England by the Luftwaffe had driven even English hopes of being able to stop Hitler to a new low. Italy had scuttled to the spurious safety of "neutrality" and nine months later, believing she saw the handwriting on the wall, had declared war. Harassed and beaten, the armies of England and France had taken defeat after defeat until Pétain had thrown in the sponge an appallingly brief period after France entered the war. Never in history had a military machine moved so speedily and destructively in so short a time. Hitler ruled from the northernmost tip of Europe down through the Italian colonies in Africa, and there was no ray of hope that the end of his conquests was in sight.

White France having toppled like a house of cards, to ask what black France could do in the face of the Nazi juggernaut would have evoked laughter had any person in those bleak days thought the Africans could do anything.

When France fell, French West Africa, Morocco, Algeria, Syria, and Indo-China followed Pétain and Laval into the arms of Hitler. There was a powerful pro-Nazi, Flemish party in the Belgian Congo; the enemy also virtually controlled the old German Southwest Africa, and other parts of South Africa. The so-called Italian Armistice Commission, backed by Marshal Graziani's Libyan Army and the Duke of Aosta's Italian Army in Ethiopia, worked under Nazi direction to effect virtually complete control by Germany and Italy of Africa from Casablanca south to the Cape of Good Hope, and eastward from Morocco to the Middle East. The Mediterranean was almost wholly in enemy hands.

Had not Hitler's plans been foiled and control of West and Central Africa thereby retained by the Allies, the consequences to the United States might have been appalling. "The presence of the Germans at Dakar," Philippe Barrès writes, "would have been for the United States a catastrophe parallel to their presence at Vladivostok." Control of the west coast of Africa would have permitted Hitler to use the ports of French Equatorial Africa and French West Africa as bases for the French and German fleets to harass American and British shipping in the South Atlantic. He would have controlled sea and air routes between Dakar and Natal in Brazil. "The day when the 'Franco-German' societies administer those lines of transport, the Italian-German penetration of Africa would be an accomplished fact and the German penetration of South America would be about to become a reality," said Barrès. With that accomplished, Hitler planned to conquer Brazil and the rest of South America by propaganda and physical force, consolidate control of sea and air in the South Atlantic and thereby isolate the United States, attack the Panama Canal and thus block our fleets from moving from the Atlantic to the Pacific. Then Germany and Japan intended jointly to attack the United States directly. This "strategy of the avalanche" may seem in 1944 fantastic and unrealizable; in 1940 it did not seem so. It was nearer to accomplishment than many Americans even now realize. Had Germany and Italy gained mastery of West and Central Africa, it could have happened. Had Eboué been Pétain or Laval, it would have happened.

The British Resident Minister in French West Africa, Lord Philip Swinton, stated when he visited Brazzaville in February 1944:

I saw M. Félix Eboué. He is one of those glorious Frenchmen who were the first to carry on even though they had but a broken sword. I remember with emotion those tragic days in 1940 when England was alone, face to face with Germany. Without doubt we had to have courage then. But those Frenchmen who decided to carry on the fight had to have even more. They were being told "England will be beaten in several weeks; you must follow the Marshal [Pétain]; obey the orders of the government, and respect the armistice." . . . France may be proud of such men.

Denis Saurat, director of the Institut Français of London, who was sent by the Free French to Equatorial Africa to assist in the organization of secondary teaching, wrote a book on his mission, *Watch Over Africa*, in which he said of Eboué, "He was the first Governor to join De Gaulle and he gave the white race an example of integrity, courage and decision that will go down the centuries to the honor of the black races and to the honor of that France that gave them their chance."

The sole territory on either the northern or western coast of Africa still held by the Allies where supplies could be landed was Nigeria. Without planes, guns, food, ammunition, and medical supplies the Middle East could not possibly hold out. The only other alternative was shipment by boat from the United States or England down the west coast of Africa, around the Cape of Good Hope, and up the east coast of Africa to the Red Sea. Even if ships succeeded in negotiating this long and perilous voyage, they were in grave danger as they passed Djibouti in Italian Somaliland at the narrow entrance between the Gulf of Aden and the Red Sea. This was a twelve-thousand-mile trip to the Middle East, requiring from six to eight weeks from Nigeria, if that territory could be held by the Allies, which seemed virtually impossible. At that time German submarines and German raiders like the *Graf Spee* infested the South Atlantic, constituting an almost insuperable hazard to Allied shipping.

The sole Allied hope of transporting supplies and men to the Middle East and averting disaster was French Equatorial Africa and, in particular, the province of Chad. In Chad's capital, Fort-Lamy, one of the largest and most modern airports in the Eastern Hemisphere had been built under Governor Eboué's administration. Also largely due to his efforts two roads had been built, one of them seventeen-hundred miles and the other two thousand miles in length, stone-surfaced for much of their length to permit their use during the rainy season when rain falls in torrents and continuously.

"If Eboué had followed the example of Pétain, Laval and Weygand, disaster would have followed," General Sicé declared. "Because he did not do so, British and American planes were landed and assembled at Nigeria, flown eastward through Fort-Lamy to Khartoum in the Anglo-Egyptian Sudan, thence northward to the Middle East. Had there been a day's delay, nothing could have stopped Hitler!"

Had not Eboué made the decision which kept Central Africa out of Hitler's control, North Africa could not have been recaptured by the Allies as soon as was the case. It follows that, if Allied landings at Casablanca, Oran and Algiers and the subsequent successful North African campaign had not been achieved, the Allies would not have gained a base from which to attack Hitler's Europe. It is possible, even probable, that the sheer weight of numbers and war production of the Allies, and particularly of the United States, would eventually have enabled the Allies to take North Africa, but the victory would have been far more costly in human lives, money, material, and time. It is a conservative estimate that World War II has been shortened months, if not years, by Eboué. But when Roosevelt, Churchill, and De Gaulle met in Casablanca in January 1943, the man who was more than any other responsible for their being able to meet in Africa, Félix Eboué, was conspicuously absent. Was it because of the color of his skin?

Here is the story told me a few weeks later by Eboué himself. There was not the slightest sign that he considered his action either heroic or unusual.

"We were sitting around the radio in the military club

at Fort-Lamy the night of June 17, 1940, to listen to Pétain's broadcast. With me were young French Army officers, graduates of Saint-Cyr, several of the department heads and other officials of Chad, and some of the local merchants and functionaries. When Pétain had finished, a great silence, born of great pain, fell upon us all. But that pain was assuaged for me because I sensed that all Chad stood together in its determination not to yield. Two nights later we again assembled to listen to the broadcasts by Churchill and De Gaulle from London. I did not then know De Gaulle and had heard little about him. But when he declared that France had lost a battle but not a war, my mind was made up. I proposed to those gathered about the radio that we serve notice that, whatever the cost, we would continue to fight. I gave them a choice: to follow Vichy or De Gaulle. All but a few chose De Gaulle. About thirty elderly French merchants and officials decided to leave, but nine of them had a change of heart a short distance from Chad and returned.

"By a clandestine method we dispatched to De Gaulle in London on June 26 a cable telling him that all Chad believed that he and not Vichy represented the honor of France and that he could count to the limit on Chad. When no reply was received from him, we again cabled him, on July 7, renewing our pledge of support and our determination to fight both Vichy and Germany. We told him what Chad could contribute in soldiers, funds, minerals, and other supplies. This time he cabled, 'Await my instructions.' "

It was later learned why the June 26 cable had not been answered. It had been sent in the French-British code for May 1940, because a later code had not then been received in Chad. When the cable reached England, the British were unable to decode it. When, however, the cable of July 7 was received, it occurred to some Englishman to consult the codes for previous months. The two messages then became clear and were delivered to De Gaulle.

But Eboué had not, in the meantime, been idle. The province of Gabon was first to follow Chad in declaring for De Gaulle; but a few days later it reversed its decision and declared for Vichy. The provinces of Ubangi and Middle Congo, persuaded by Eboué, declared against Vichy and stood firm. Completely cut off from the world by Vichy censorship but knowing of the tragic success of German conquests, they knew that they would have to stand alone. They were aware that Pétain and the others who had formed the puppet Vichy government had done so because of their conviction that the fall of Britain was inevitable and that a Nazi-dominated Europe, and perhaps a Nazi-dominated world, was inevitable. But the hopeless outlook did not discourage them.

Pierre Boisson was Governor-General of French Equatorial Africa when France fell. He was at first determined to continue resistance to Germany. But when Vichy appointed him commissioner of all of "Black Africa" in July 1940, with headquarters at Dakar, he reversed his position and entered the camp of Vichy. Pierre Husson, then Acting Governor-General and commanding general of the troops of French Equatorial Africa, and Governor Masson of Gabon completely and vigorously cast in their lot with Vichy. The outlook became even darker each succeeding day, until late in August, when René Pleven was dispatched by De Gaulle by plane from London to Fort-Lamy.

De Gaulle and a few who had escaped from France to London were then alone, an almost pathetic government in exile without resources or territory from which to operate. French West Africa had gone Vichy; Indo-China had fallen into the hands of Japan; the mother country having fallen into control of the enemy, one by one France's colonies, with the exception of Equatorial Africa, had been lost.

Eboué's eyes sparkled as he told of Pleven's arrival in Fort-Lamy on August 23, 1940. Pleven had not been able to send word that he was coming. But Eboué, by the mysterious grapevine of Africa, had learned from Lagos that Pleven was on the way. Eboué ordered the people of Fort-Lamy to turn out in welcome. When Pleven saw the crowd gathered at the Fort-Lamy airport, he was not sure whether they were friend or foe. He had had no news of what changes might have taken place. At last, because there was nothing else he could do, since there was no other airport within many miles nor sufficient gasoline to reach it had there been one, Pleven ordered the plane to descend. As he stepped forth somewhat uncertainly, the huge crowd burst into cheers. Pleven sighed with relief as Eboué stepped forward to welcome him.

Natives of Fort-Lamy and surrounding territories of Chad appeared at Government House to present money in response to De Gaulle's appeal for funds to assist the underground movement in France. The sums were small—but all had given. The poorer black natives gave, in proportion to their resources, even more than the white merchants. Civil servants contributed a month's salary. Members of the Association of Blind Beggars—there is much blindness in that part of Africa due to the terrific sandstorms—gave their mites, earned by making wicker baskets. The eyes of Pleven at Algiers became moist when he told me shortly afterward of the donations to help France free herself.

Early in 1944 it was announced that the natives of French West African colonies had contributed more than a hundred and forty-three million French francs to the French resistance movement.

The importance of Eboué's decision was generously acknowledged by De Gaulle. Philippe Barrès, in his book on De Gaulle, quotes De Gaulle's stirring citation in awarding the Order of the Empire to Chad:

The enemy thought to have done with France by imposing an abominable armistice. The enemy was fooled. Others imagined that France definitely would fight no more. These gentlemen have committed an error.

France has been temporarily struck down by a form of warfare for which she was not prepared. In its distress our country doubted itself. She doubted her allies. Certain Frenchmen, blinded by despair, managed to forget two thousand years of history and persuade themselves that the road to salvation lay in submission to Hitler and Mussolini.

How could they? France is France. She has within her a secret strength that has always astounded the world and has not yet ceased to astound it. Though crushed, humiliated, and surrendered, France is beginning to climb up the slopes of the abyss.

The Frenchmen of Chad have just given proof of it. Spontaneously these upright, sane, brave men have taken up their arms and are going into battle. I have reason to believe that others will follow their example.

I have reason to say that a fighting France is in process of reformation. Her forces are increasing. I have reason to believe that there is still honor and glory for France. I have reason to assure you that since she remains present in the war France will be present at the victory.

Today, August 27, 1940, the three hundred and sixtieth day of the World War, I bestow the order of the Empire on the territory of Chad on the following grounds:

Under the inspiration of its leaders, Governor Eboué and

Colonel Marchand, military commandant of the territory, Chad has demonstrated that it has remained first and foremost a land of valiant Frenchmen.

Despite an unusually dangerous military and economic situation, Chad has refused to subscribe to a shameful surrender and has resolved to pursue the war to its victorious conclusion. By its admirable resolution it has shown the road of duty and given the signal of rehabilitation to the whole French empire.

Because De Gaulle's French has the nuances and eloquence of the spoken instead of the written French, which is difficult to translate adequately, the text of his citation is included:

L'ennemi a cru que par l'abominable armistice il en avait fini avec la France. L'ennemi s'est trompé. Dans le monde, des gens se sont imaginés que, décidément, la France ne se battrait plus. Ces gens ont commis une erreur.

La France s'est trouvée momentanément foudroyée par une forme de guerre qu'elle n'avait pas préparée. Dans son malheur notre pays a pu douter de lui-même. Il a pu douter de ses alliés. Certains Français, aveuglés par le désespoir, ont pu oublier deux mille ans d'histoire et penser que la voie de salut était la soumission à Hitler et à Mussolini.

Mais quoi? La France est la France. Il y a en elle un ressort secret qui, depuis toujours, étonna le monde et qui n'a pas fini de l'éttoner. La France écrasée, humiliée, livrée, commence a remonter la pente de l'abîme.

Les Français du Tchad viennent d'en donner la preuve. Spontanément ces hommes droits, ces hommes sains, ces hommes braves reprennent leurs armes et vont au combat. J'ai des raisons de penser que leur example sera suivi.

J'ai des raisons de dire qu'il se reforme une France combattante, dont les forces vont croissant. J'ai des raisons de croire qu'il y a encore de l'honneur et de la gloire pour la France. J'ai des raisons d'affirmer qu'en demeurant présente à la bataille, la France sera présente à la victoire.

Aujourd'hui, 27 août 1940, 360 e jour de la guerre mondiale, je cite a l'ordre de l'Empire le territoire du Tchad pour le motif suivant:

Sous l'impulsion de ses chefs, le Gouverneur Eboué et le Colonel Marchand, commandant militaire du territoire, le Tchad a montré qu'il demeurait par excellence une terre de Français vaillants.

En dépit d'une situation militaire et économique particulièrement dangereuse, le territoire du Tchad a refusé de souscrire à une capitulation honteuse et décidé de poursuivre la guerre, jusqu'à la victoire. Par son admirable résolution, a montré le chemin du devoir et donné le signal du redressement à l'empire français tout entier.

But Chad, and later all of French Equatorial Africa, when the pro-Vichy officials had been ousted, contributed far more than the voluntary contributions of individuals to the Allied cause. As speedily as manpower and materials permitted, the harbors of Pointe-Noire, Duala, Libreville, and Port Gentil were developed to handle the greatly needed volume of war materials. The production of rubber was trebled. The production of tin, lead, zinc, and other materials was greatly increased. The volume of production of cotton, coffee, peanut and palm oil, cocoa, and wood to be shipped for use by Allied armies was immeasurably increased.

Eboué's preparation for the role he was destined to play in France's and the world's crisis was characteristic of the determination and courage he exhibited when France collapsed. He was born December 26, 1884, at Cayenne, French Guiana. Sent by his parents to France, he graduated from the Bordeaux Lycée, and then enrolled in the French School of Colonial Sciences. Though born in the Western Hemisphere, Eboué's major interest was Africa. He asked to be assigned to that continent and in 1911 was sent as a minor civil servant to Chad. He was not content to live the life of relative ease in his job, but chose to travel by whatever means were available, most of them then of the most primitive sort, to every part not only of Chad but of French Equatorial Africa. He thereby learned to know the people and the natural resources and also to be known and respected by the natives. Two decades later, in 1930, he became chief colonial administrator of a district of Ubangi-Shari. Vested now with augmented power, he began extensively and vigorously to put into effect agricultural, administrative, and other innovations and reforms. He was the first to recommend the cultivation of cotton in the upper Ubangi, the raising and improvement in quality of that cotton having materially added to the economic prosperity of that territory. Under his administration roads, schools, hospitals, and other facilities to raise the living standards and to improve the economic status of the natives were built. Pestilent areas where malaria, sleeping sickness, and other dread diseases of the tropics had from time immemorial exacted a heavy toll of life were cleaned up. The number of native medical assistants to serve the vast territory was increased, largely by his efforts, from two hundred to thirty-six hundred. Midwives were given instructions in the aiding of childbirth to replace the primitive methods of delivery.

But Eboué, despite all he had done, was far from content when I talked with him at Cairo. Little knowing, either of us, that he was destined to die before he could return to his beloved Equatorial Africa, he said to me with great earnestness, "We must declare war on illness; we must abolish poverty and ignorance. It is not enough to put more money in the pockets of the natives. We must end the robbing of the natives by big planters and companies who are determined to continue colonial exploitation. French Equatorial Africa needs doctors, technicians, teachers, scientists to help develop its people and its resources. And we are going to get them," he added with determination.

One of Governor Eboué's most interesting contributions, in which he was assisted by Mme. Eboué, an accomplished musician, was a study made by them of the primitive telegraphic system—the tom-tom. They published a book, *The Tom-Tom Language of Ubangi*, in which was demonstrated that the notes of the tom-tom form an exact counterpart of a spoken language. The notes of the tom-tom were fitted to the tonic scale of Western music by the Eboués so that Africans and non-Africans could understand and utilize it in areas where telegraph wires did not yet exist.

Jean de la Roche, for seven years *chef de cabinet* to Governor-General Eboué in Guadeloupe and French Equatorial Africa, tells this story of how Eboué checked the accuracy of his adaptation of the notes of the tom-tom to the piano. One day shortly after Governor and Mme. Eboué discovered that the notes of the tom-tom language could be reproduced on the piano, he tried it out by calling to his servants, "Come here quickly!" playing the notes on the piano. Almost instantaneously the doors of the room burst open as servants came running in, almost startled out of their wits.

M. de la Roche reveals in another story the warm humanness of Eboué. On one occasion when General de Gaulle and his wife were dining with Eboué and his wife at the palace in Brazzaville, the Governor sighed deeply. Thinking his sadness was due to preoccupation with affairs of state,

De Gaulle asked Eboué why he sighed. The Governor-General answered, "I am thinking that it is a great tragedy that I must spend my life as a second-rate administrator when, if I were free and had the time, I would be one of the world's great cooks."

In addition to the scholarly book written by the Governor and Mme. Eboué on the tom-tom, his *Native Policy in Equatorial Africa* is one of the ablest inquiries into colonial administration and the condition of Africans which has been written. In the last state document Eboué was destined to write *"d'A.E.F. et la guerre,"* a report on the Administrative Council of French Equatorial Africa, Governor Eboué in academy French of great beauty and clarity explained the condition of French Equatorial Africa in its relation to France and to the world, concisely reported on his administration during 1943, and set forth plans and proposed budget for 1944.

One item in that budget is both interesting and revealing: though the number of doctors for civilian population had been cut in half by the war, the expenditure for medical services had been increased from 19,900,000 francs in 1939 to 60,500,000 francs in 1940. Included in his program were plans for the extension of agriculture, manufacturing, shipping, production of war metals desperately needed by the Allies, and for the further development of Radio Brazzaville which, during the Hitler occupation of Europe, supplied the world with much of its war and other news. It is doubtful whether such a report by a colonial administrator, its central emphasis being the welfare of the people, has ever before been written.

For nine years, beginning in 1930, Eboué was successively Secretary-General of the Sudan and then Governor pro tem of the Sudan, later Secretary-General and Governor pro tem of Martinique, and was appointed Governor of Guadeloupe in December 1936. The governorship of Guadeloupe in the West Indies, at the time of Eboué's appointment to it in 1936, was one of the most eagerly sought posts in French colonial administration. With high hopes, based upon the liberalism then sweeping France, he set out for his new post. He took literally the ideals of the French Popular Front government of Léon Blum. In Guadeloupe Eboué initiated promptly and vigorously significant social reforms, including higher wages, better housing, improved social conditions, and trade-unionism for native labor. He became, naturally, a hero to native labor, but anathema to the colonial planters whose wealth was built upon the sugar industry which dominated the island's economy. Vigorous and repeated demands were made upon Paris to recall "this dangerous Red."

Before senatorial elections at the end of 1938, Eboué was abruptly summoned to Paris "for consultation" by the Minister of Colonies, Georges Mandel. The Minister of Colonies attempted to persuade Governor Eboué to use his power in behalf of one of Mandel's friends who was a candidate for the Senate. Eboué bluntly refused to do so because he did not believe that, as Governor, he should interfere with the free choice by the people of their elected representatives. Mandel was angered by Eboué's decision and refused to permit him to return to Guadeloupe as Governor, sending him instead to Chad. Assignment of Eboué to Chad was considered by the defenders of conservative French colonial policy as banishment and punishment. Little did they realize that in sending Eboué to Equatorial Africa, at the behest of the Guadeloupe sugar planters because he was practicing democracy there, they were casting him in a role in which he was destined to play a decisive part in saving democracy all over the world.

Life had been most comfortable in Guadeloupe, Eboué told me, and he had been reluctant to accept the transfer. He had asked time to think it over. He and Mme. Eboué had eventually, but with some reluctance, decided that it was their duty to undertake the task in Africa, which was even then appalling in its difficulties and complexities. Though entitled to eight months' vacation, he and Mme. Eboué left by plane the following day for Africa.

Shortly before his death Eboué had the satisfaction of seeing at least the beginning of a more liberal colonial policy for his people as reward for their loyalty to France and to the Allies. Late in January 1944 there assembled in Brazzaville, with Governor-General Eboué as the host, a conference on colonial policy at which were present the governors, administrators, and technicians of the French colonies in Africa south of the Sahara. De Gaulle flew to the Brazzaville Conference from Algiers to address the opening session. The North African territories of French Morocco, Algeria, and Tunisia were not represented, presumably because Morocco and Tunisia were protectorates instead of colonies while Algeria is regarded as part of France. The sub-Sahara colonies represented constituted 3,450,000 of the 4,617,579 square miles of the French colonial empire; its 25,000,000 inhabitants more than one third of the 70,000,000 French colonials.

It was made clear that France expects and is determined to hold on to her colonies, but there was a sharp reversal of French colonial policy which, if put into effect, may affect materially the policy of all colonial powers. René Pleven, in his capacity as Minister of Colonies, asserted that the New France, if and when restored, would reject the philosophy that colonies were for the sole purpose of furnishing raw materials and manpower. Tentative plans to improve education of natives were discussed; as, for example, the creation of an Institute of Social Hygiene and research for the education of doctors, particularly in tropical diseases, botanists, entomologists, and geologists. Special training for the education of natives as colonial administrators was proposed. Frenchmen from metropolitan France are to be given special training and charged with the responsibility of working to improve the status of the natives instead of devoting their energies to the benefit of planters and absentee landlords. It was urged that the colonies not only participate in the drafting of the new French constitution, but that they should participate in the administration of the affairs of France to a greater degree than has been true in the past. The abolition of the conscription of labor was recommended, though there appears to be a joker in the substitution of a tax to be paid by the natives in money *or labor*. The poverty of many natives has been so great in the African colonies that the majority of them actually receive in cash as little or less than American sharecroppers.

Trade-unionism for natives was discussed, though the governors and administrators resolved that conditions were such that native labor would have no need of trade unions for some time to come. But at least the concept of colonials joining trade unions was envisioned.

A modified recognition of the tribal organization of French colonies and other parts of Africa and a limited citizenship for natives able to meet certain qualifications were considered and recommended.

In terms of the Four Freedoms and the proclamations of the Allied nations that World War II is being fought for the "freedom of all men everywhere," the deliberations and recommendations of the Brazzaville Conference were limited. It was made clear to me by M. Pleven and other officials of the FCNL that the putting into effect of these recommendations must wait until metropolitan France has been restored. "France will need all her trained men," M. Pleven said, "to rebuild France before she can spare any to institute reforms in the colonies."

M. Eboué was aware, when I talked with him in Cairo, of this delay. He was also aware of the pressure which other colonial powers, once the war ended and the danger of defeat had passed, would bring to bear upon a France struggling to rise again as a world power to soft-pedal the issue of colonial reforms. I asked him if his plans for French Equatorial Africa included eventual abolition of the colonial system and empire based on such systems, which would mean complete independence and freedom for the natives of Africa. His response was both prompt and disappointing. "We are Frenchmen," he said, "and we are loyal to France."

Proudly he told me—not as a Negro Frenchman but as a citizen of France—of more than a hundred and fifty Allied planes a day passing through the Fort-Lamy airport between June and September 1940, transporting air-borne troops and supplies to the Middle East. He told me the story of the recruitment and training of African troops who marched seventeen hundred grueling miles across the Sahara to fight valiantly in Tripoli and Tunisia. Some of Eboué's soldiers were among the first Allied troops to enter Paris as a part of the 2nd French Armored Division.

Eboué's three sons were then and are now fighting in the French Army. Henri, the eldest, had fought in the Battle of France, had been a prisoner for eighteen months in a Nazi prison camp from which he had escaped and made his way to Tunisia, where he was then serving in the French Army.

Robert, twenty-four, had also been captured and had escaped; Eboué had no news of him for six months except a German broadcast that he had escaped. Charles, the youngest, had earned his civilian pilot license in an aviation school in Canada at the age of seventeen, had enlisted, and was now flying as a pilot in the Fighting French Army. Henri and Robert, after escaping from German prison camps, had made their way to Vichy, where they eluded capture until they had found their sister. One of Pétain's staff had cabled Eboué, "Remember your children," as a thinly veiled threat to force him to pledge allegiance to Vichy. This was in June 1940. Henri and Robert, therefore, knew their peril as fugitives in Vichy. But with the aid of the British consul at Barcelona the three had made their way to Lisbon, and from there to Brazzaville. Thus the courage of the parents seems to have been handed down to sons and daughter.

This, then, is the saga of a black man in Central Africa into whose hands was placed the decision upon which depended the answer to the question of whether or not the world would be ruled by a Nazi master-race domination or by an imperfect democracy.

Chapter Twelve

No GREATER HOPE for the eventual solution of the tangled race issue can be found than in those instances where some white Americans have shown that their democracy rises above prejudice and ignorance. It is unfortunate that such examples as are given are isolated in a welter of ready acceptance or practice of prejudice. But they demonstrate that there is a reservoir of decency and democracy which, unfortunately, some of the high officials of the Army and Navy neither recognize nor encourage. Many, many times as many episodes of directly opposite content and spirit could, unhappily, be cited. But throughout the history of mankind it has always been true that a minority has clung to ideals and thereby kept the struggle for freedom from fading from the earth. The postwar years will see which philosophy is to dominate America and the world—that of those who have spread hate at home and overseas or of Americans who really believe in democracy and practice it.

Three white American soldiers sat in front seats in a crowded bus in Florida one hot summer day in 1944. A wounded Negro veteran, wearing the service stripes of the Tunisian, Sicilian, and Italian campaigns, boarded the bus. One of the white soldiers got up and offered the Negro soldier his seat as there were no vacant seats. The bus driver told the veteran he could not sit in the seat but would have to move to the rear where Florida law provided Negroes must sit. The white soldier pointed out to the driver that there were no vacant seats. The driver replied angrily that the Negro would have to go back anyway, as "niggers can't sit up front in Florida."

The white soldier turned to his buddies and asked, "Does he sit or doesn't he?"

"He does!" a roar assured him.

The white soldier turned again to the red-faced driver to tell him, "Either he sits down and you drive on or we'll throw you off the bus and I'll drive!"

The Negro veteran remained in his seat and the bus drove on.

A few weeks later a similar though somewhat less dramatic episode occurred in Maryland. When a group of white Marines entered a bus between T.B., Maryland, and Warsaw, Virginia, the driver ordered three Negro passengers to move to the back and sit behind the Marines. The latter told the driver they could easily find seats in another part of the vehicle and that he need not disturb himself. One made the remark, "This must be the South!" When the driver grew angry and belligerent, the Marines became adamant and refused to let the Negro passengers move. The driver abruptly decided to practice discretion instead of valor.

The Army and Marine Corps hold no monopoly, however. During the Detroit race riots in 1943 three sailors waded into a white mob which was beating unmercifully a slender Negro youth. "He isn't doing you guys any harm. Let him alone!" one of the trio shouted as he and his companions rescued the Negro and fought back the mob.

"What's it to you?" one of the rioters snarled.

"Plenty," replied the sailor. "There was a colored guy in our outfit in the Pacific and he saved the lives of two of my buddies. Besides, you guys are stirring up here at home something we are fighting to stop!"

In contrast to the actions of the home folks, many Detroiters in the armed services both abroad and in American camps were unsparing in their condemnation of the riots. One of the best of these protests was a letter to a Detroit newspaper from an indignant and bewildered group of Detroit servicemen who wrote home:

Why are these race riots going on there in Detroit and in other cities in this land—supposedly the land of freedom, equality and brotherhood?

We who are doing the fighting, and will do the fighting to preserve this country from such acts of discrimination; we who recognize no discrimination in the trenches and fox-holes; we shed the same blood—one kind of blood—red. Things like race riots and strikes make us fighters think—*what are we fighting for?*

Americanism means everything to us, but it is swiftly turning to be an unfounded word. Regardless, we will continue to fight, to die for our loved ones. But we want to feel and know that we are fighting for the principles that gave birth to the United States of America.

In this hospital ward, we eat, laugh, and sleep uncomplainingly together. Jim Stanley, Negro; Joe Wakamatau, Japanese; Eng Yu, Chinese; John Brennan, Irish; Paul Colosi, Italian; Don Holzheimer, German; Joe Wojiechowski, Polish; and Mike Cohen, Jewish.

We were all injured in the line of duty. Yes—Hitler, Mussolini, Hirohito, all rub their fists in glee that their fifth column work of undermining our country is bearing fruit. Things like this prolong the war, and give the Axis time to strengthen their forces. They might possibly mean *defeat* for us. Now more than ever we should pull together, and work side by side, unhampered by riots and strikes. We want to know that you are behind us 100 per cent. We want to know you want us back regardless of creed, race or color.

We want to know so that we can fight harder and, if need be, die willingly.

Another encouraging sign of the inherent decency of American soldiers was reported in *Collier's* magazine by Ashton Reid in an article on *Yank*, the servicemen's magazine. Mr. Reid wrote:

Yank doesn't give much space to the usual Army gripes which have been going on for centuries anyway and are merely rediscovered in each war. But it isn't afraid to tackle a social problem. There was the case of the Negro corporal who was forced to eat in a railroad restaurant kitchen in the South, while German prisoners of war ate in the dining room. GIs rushed in from all over to bawl out officialdom for this and to ask, "Is this what we're fighting for?"

From the Marianas a staff sergeant, a Southerner, dismayed by the treatment of his Negro fellow soldiers, recently wrote me:

We have fought one of our enemies and they went down in disastrous defeat. We have another enemy. It is the attempt to "hold back" the colored people of the United States. When I return to North Carolina after the war I am going to fight for the betterment of those colored folks. I am a white fellow but I am a Christian who deeply feels the colored folks as a whole, if educated, can gain their rightful *equal rights*. [Italics are his.] Would you advise me as to the course I can take to get into a position to really help them?

Or there is the case of Sergeant Frank Batterson, Air Corps gunner in a B-17 which was shot down over Germany by a squadron of Focke-Wulf 190s. Here is his story as he told it to a San Francisco reporter.

To give coherency to his belief, Batterson went back to the day he lost his leg. It was in January of 1943. His B-17 accomplished its bombing mission over a French target and was en route back to England when the entire formation was attacked by a squadron of German FW-190s.

"We fell out of formation with two engines hit and battled till everything went out, even our intercommunication system.

"The pilot tried to bring the ship back but couldn't. Then he found that the bail-out bell had gone. He gave verbal orders to abandon the plane but I stayed at my guns. Then a piece of shrapnel tore through the plane and ripped off my leg.

"I looked at it and realized that I didn't have much more to lose so after firing a few more rounds I bailed out. Fortunately the leg strap of the 'chute became a kind of tourniquet, halting the flow of blood. I must have passed out because the next thing I knew I was in a hospital in Brittany, under German military guard, but with French doctors and sisters taking care of me."

An amputated right leg and seventeen months in a Nazi prison camp followed, of which Sergeant Batterson said:

"I saw girls honored because of their pure 'Aryan' blood, segregated into special maternity camps for breeding purposes and watched them strut in their special uniforms. They were about fourteen years old.

"Every week I read the German-published prison newspaper *O.K.* Ninety per cent of it was anti-Semitic propaganda and the rest was anti-Negro and anti-British and anti-Roosevelt.

"Then I came home and found those same forces at work here. It was the same propaganda—the same attempt to divide by hate and fear and the promoting of differences.

"Let me tell you one thing, the men fighting over there, and particularly the ones whom I knew in the prison camps, know what they're fighting for. They've gained that knowledge through bitter experience and they understand the basic issues involved in this war.

"Among the several thousand prisoners there in the prison camp, our problems were common. We were Chinese and Japanese and Negro. We were Protestant and Catholic and Jewish. But first we were American, and that's what we expected to find at home, that same kind of unity built and made stronger out of small differences.

"But instead, what is there? There is an increase in anti-Semitism. There are race riots. There are at large here all those forces which created Nazism. For I have learned that if we withhold rights from one group we'll withhold freedom from all Americans.

"And there is no question in my mind that here at home we have two choices. We can close our eyes to the evil forces that are being bred here, or we can acknowledge the situation and fight it before it reaches its inevitable conclusion.

"The Germans once had the same choice and took the first and became Nazis. And we'll fall into the same pit unless we take heed—and action—now."

A Navy ensign, the son of wealthy New York parents, was so shocked by the racial attitude in the service that he sent a full month's pay to the National Association for the Advancement of Colored People, saying, "I always intended to contribute to your organization but never felt so strongly about the matter as since I came in contact with the attitude of the officers of our Navy." He added that many of the officers he encountered delighted in telling "Negro" jokes such as, "One of the instructors explained in detail how to legally avoid hiring Negroes for civilian Navy jobs! If a Negro were in the class the instructor would be too embarrassed to do these things—and his realization of the sense of embarrassment would be a healthy thing. I sometimes wish that the law which prohibits making false claims for commercial products also prohibited making false claims for our democracy (that is, 'without regard to race, creed, or color')."

What is the soil from which such attitudes grow? Here is part of the answer in a letter received in 1943 from a Northern soldier in a Southern training camp. He writes of the impact of the South's attitude toward the Negro on Northern soldiers.

I have been in somewhat of an advantageous position to observe this as I have been an instructor in the Army Air Force for the past six months, during all that period stationed here in Southern Florida.

As you may know, this is the largest Air Force Basic Training Center in the United States. Newly inducted draftees who have been assigned to the Air Force are sent here for their basic military training. As a Flight Leader, I am assigned to flights of 64 men each, live with these men and teach them until their basic training is completed.

It is true, it seems to me, that the initial reaction of young Northern soldiers down here is one of shocked surprise at the more rank forms of discrimination. For instance, I remember that when I first came down here, a group of us men were shocked to see separate seats for Negro passengers in the buses. On more than one occasion I have seen (and myself have done it) white soldiers get up from their seats in the front of the bus and *insist* that standing Negro women sit down. The soldiers were very firm about this and the few white Southerners present kept their mouths shut if they didn't like it.

For my own small part, I do what I can in my talks with these new men to show them that he who holds prejudice against his fellow countrymen because their skin color happens to be different—such a soldier is directly helping the enemy he may give his life in battle to defeat. In my own mind the question is as simple as all that. Under the heading of "Army Orientation" I get several occasions to discuss current affairs and give a large portion of this time to answering specific points of prejudice which these men have. However, I don't know of any other instructors doing this.

Regretfully, I must add that I have seen a good number of Northern soldiers pick up some of the bigotry of the South. Inasmuch as we soldiers here have absolutely no contact with the Negro people ourselves, this intolerance takes the form of use of the usual "hate words"—"nigger," et cetera.

I have thought about this phenomenon at length and my own feeling is that this is caused by the complete lack of contact between white and Negro soldiers (and civilians too, of course). Up North, we got to know each other, a little bit, anyway, but here the Army keeps all Negroes out, perhaps fearing they might "contaminate" the elite hotels in which we are quartered. What balderdash!

I recall as a civilian we thought that the Army's Jim Crow policy was bad, among other reasons, because it continued existing Jim Crow policies. But it is far worse than that because in some persons, it is putting prejudice where none existed before. This policy I hope will be broken down by public protests, and if the Army takes a first step in a more *American* direction by forming a mixed squadron in the Air Force (Technical Training Command) I will certainly volunteer for it.

A Long Island businessman shares a letter from his younger brother, who wrote of his dismay in this fashion:

I was going to write you yesterday but I was kept plenty busy with the GI Party, and with preparations for our forthcoming hike. What I want to tell you about is the extremely heated argument between a few Southern boys and a few Northern lads over the Negro situation which ended in a flurry of fisticuffs when one of the Southern boys thought he could hit my friend and get away with it. He didn't. But that is running away with myself.

I am really amazed at the extreme unintelligence of a Southern lad, college graduate or not. I have the utmost contempt for the South and its educational system. After hearing stories of how Negroes are treated—our Corporal was *proud* to tell us the following story:

"There was a Negro soldier who sat in a bus, but not in the back where he should have. The bus driver told him to move. He didn't. The bus driver called a cop who told him to move. He still didn't. The cop, with the utmost contempt for the uniform of a U.S. soldier, shot him through the head."

The boy relating this story to me then was proud to say, and this burned me up, that nothing happened to the cop, for the simple reason that the "Nigger" should have known his place. When I ask him how anybody has the right to make a place for another person, he can't answer. When I ask him exactly what he is fighting for, he says, "freedom!" Then I say, "Well, Corp, if you're fighting for freedom, then why don't you practice what you preach as far as the Negroes of the South are concerned?" He doesn't say much except that the Negroes of the South are happy. I say, "Do they know any better?"

He also said that he would rather salute a stump of wood with an officer's uniform on than a Negro officer. He claims that if he ever had to salute a Negro officer, he would kill him if he ever met him after the war. And he had two years of college.

We then went on to discuss the educational system in the South. There is where the fisticuffs came in. My friend said that he couldn't imagine that the educational system was worth much if they couldn't teach a few practices of democracy and many things to that effect. The Southern boy then thought that he might as well defend the "honor" of the South and started swinging. It was soon broken up.

———, in my personal opinion, they can have my uniform. I'm not proud of it now, not when I can meet so many people who, in their own way, practice Fascism. Maybe I'm wrong in thinking so. I hope I'm wrong in your eyes, for it is bad for a young fellow to think about one part of his country as I do. I feel better towards the South and the Southern boys. I used to think that when one talked about the Civil War being fought all over again, that it was a gag. Not any more, for I just came away from the Battle of Gettysburg—I'm not kidding.

Sunday Morn.

We had another discussion about the Negro situation. It seems to be the big thing around here.

Some Southern boys do believe that a Negro should be treated as a man. They say, "Give them education, give them all the rights we have, but always remember that a white man is always better than a colored man." They say, "Let the white man live in one place and the colored man in another."

It all adds up to one thing, that a boy runs into a brick wall when he talks to a Southern boy about the Negro. No matter how intelligent that boy may be, a "Nigger is a Nigger" and that's all. Add that up to the already great scare of "Tradition." Yes, I've found out that that's all it is, just tradition and tradition is a hard thing to battle.

The older brother comments:

That letter was from my soldier brother, a boy of twenty. He never thought much about this, or any other social problem (or political or economic problems, for that matter). He was just an everyday boy whose friends included other everyday boys without regard to race, color, creed, religion or nationality.

But one of his best friends, a colored boy, was killed in North Africa. So, the treatment of Negroes in the South (or in the North, for that matter) doesn't quite appeal to his sense of decency and fair play.

Most Northern soldiers sent to Southern training camps, another soldier writes, "do not observe, do not care, and do not learn. They are not socially conscious and tend to accept the status quo without thought or objection." But among what he terms a very small minority the effect is marked.

Where we were very theoretically idealistic about doing away with racial prejudice before, we have become more militant. Opinions gained from reading, lectures and other impersonal and abstract sources have now been intensified and strengthened by individual contact. I speak from personal experience. Previously it was just a question of right and wrong, justice and injustice. Now that I have seen the actual living and working prejudice and its effects, it has become much more real and vital an issue to me. I have learned to hate it and am ready to fight it actively. A third group, relatively small, offers the most hope for the future. They were more or less "neutral" before, but have now been shocked and awakened by the Southern attitude toward the Negro. I believe they will form a strong sentiment for elimination of racial inequalities and prejudices after the war. One thing I definitely do not believe is that any substantial number of Northern men have succumbed to the South's traditional stupidity in this problem. Very few of the "neutral" group I mentioned above has learned to hold his colored brother in contempt. Where they have changed at all, it has been a progressive change in the direction of liberalism.

Finally, in this testimony of an enlightened minority in our armed services, there is this experience of an Army officer:

I am one of the new crop of second lieutenants who has come up from the ranks after almost two years as an enlisted man. I was born and educated in New York—and the major part of my Army career has been spent in a large training camp in a Southern state. It has been my good fortune to have been able to speak with many hundreds of soldiers, white and colored, from every portion of the country. So much for my background.

Inasmuch as limitations of time preclude the writing of an organized paper, I will set down thoughts as they occur to me:

The Jim Crow Policy of the Army. My strong impression is that the highest-ranking men in the War Department are liberal in thought and policy, reflecting the attitude of the National Administration. Evidence for this belief can be found in many aspects of Army activity which can be traced only to a definite policy: (a) Negro officer candidates; (b) One of the lecturers in Current Events at the OCS I attended was a young Negro officer who so impressed his all-white audience from thirty-eight states that, after each lecture, there was prolonged, spontaneous applause; (c) Participation of Negro soldiers as teams in organized sports programs—competition with teams of white soldiers—who, by the way, have a great deal of unconcealed respect for the athletic prowess of the Negro; (d) Careful thought and planning by responsible authorities for the recreation and welfare of Negro troops; (e) When a noted Negro singer performed at our post, Negro soldiers were seated directly behind the officers' section—a marked sign of preference, and a reversal of usual procedure; I felt that this was a mark of courtesy and consideration in a difficult situation—and the five thousand seats in the great hall were filled to overflowing; (f) In a musical revue in which I participated, there was an all-Negro act which was enthusiastically and universally hailed as the best in the show.

On the other hand, of course, due to the strong prejudices of lower-ranking officers (and some very high-ranking ones, too) with smaller minds and badly conditioned backgrounds, I was somehow made to feel that showing too markedly progressive an attitude in regard to Negroes was regarded with disfavor by The Powers That Were. One officer from the deep South recently confided to me that all this talk about equality for Negroes was Axis propaganda fiendishly designed to spread disunity! O tempora! And, of course, the sight of masses of Negro soldiers, constantly blocked off into separate groups and assigned to menial jobs generates in the mind of the average soldier a frighteningly powerful feeling of superiority and of being "different." Here are some reactions of officers and enlisted men towards Negroes:

(1) Texas. A Tech. Sgt., high-school grad, 28: "Niggers are lazy. The white man has to prove that he's boss or they won't have any respect for him. They have to be kept in their place. Sure, I believe in equality, but it's got to take a long, long time. They're only four generations removed from the African barbarians. You people up North want to change things overnight. You're heading for a revolution."

(2) Birmingham, Alabama. A corporal, high-school grad, 23; subject was the segregation of Negro blood by the Red Cross —in answer to my arguments and to *PM*'s articles, which I made him read: "If I were bleeding to death on a battlefield (he was a clerk in an office at the time) I'd rather have the blood of a maggot-infested horse than the blood of a Negro." "You're a damned liar," I told him hotly. After hours of discussion, he finally admitted that if he were actually facing death he might feel a little differently about it, and after some prodding, said that if he could be sure that everyone in his home town would agree to change his attitude towards the Negro, he'd be glad to follow suit. "Sure, I respect your sincerity," he told me, "but I don't want to be called a 'nigger-lover'!"

(3) North Carolina. A sincere, 28-year-old schoolteacher with professedly progressive inclinations (a fellow student at OCS): "Yes, we want to give the Negroes equality—in fact we work very hard in their behalf—but why mix them with whites? Give them equality of opportunity, by all means—by themselves!"

(4) Virginia. A 22-year-old high-school grad, a fellow

student at OCS: "If you're such a believer in equality for niggers, would you marry a nigger?" His question ended on a note of triumph. "What is your religion?" I asked. "Protestant," he replied. "Would you marry a Catholic?" He fell strangely silent. I thought he saw the point—that the color line is not the only barrier to miscegenation.

(5) Kansas. A 29-year-old high-school grad (fellow student at OCS): "Gosh, I just had to salute a goddamn nigger lieutenant! Boy, that burns me up!" And this, I thought regretfully, from a fellow who was really a swell guy whose thinking had been sadly misdirected.

(6) Georgia. A 24-year-old college grad (fellow student at OCS) who, in his soft, gentle drawl, told me that his eighteen months of Army service had greatly broadened his attitude towards Negroes. "Do you know," he smiled, "that in the grammar school I attended, the best students were always Negroes?" I was frankly disbelieving. "Why," I said, "the Negro in the South can't study effectively, he suffers too much from a feeling of futility and hopelessness." "What you don't see, old chap," he answered calmly, "is that they realize that to survive they must excel." My Georgian friend left me feeling more hopeful and encouraged than I had felt in a long time.

(7) Maryland. A mature officer: "Negroes are a lazy race. Where I come from we know how to treat 'em. Sure, there are some intelligent ones, but most of them are intellectually inferior to whites."

(8) Upper New York State. A 28-year-old, well-educated officer: "You tell a Negro to do something in a nice way, talk to him just as you would to a white person (Oh, Glory!) and he gets insolent!"

(9) New York City. A 25-year-old German emigrant who had fled to this country to escape anti-Semitism—he had spent six months in a concentration camp: "Yes, I know they (the Negroes) should be treated as equals but—I can't help it—they

smell funny!" My friend didn't know he was repeating Hitler's slander of the Jews as "not a water-loving race." . . .

How can this problem be solved—this problem which is now one of the greatest issues facing not only the American people, but all the peoples of the world, the great majority of whose populations are not white?

It cannot be solved by running away from it, by euphemisms, by platitudes, by quoting the Constitution, by evading the basic—stupid, perhaps—questions in the minds of millions of misguided people who have been taught since early childhood that the Negro is dirty, dull, ignorant, lazy, inferior in intellect to the whites, foul-smelling, barbaric, and everything else that is evil. These questions must be answered—answered and destroyed methodically and completely—by an overwhelming and impregnable array of irrefutable facts based on history and science and logic.

Here, then, out of their mouths is reflected the confused, vacillating, timorous policy of the high command, despite which there shines through the basic and, we hope, ineradicable faith in the democratic process. If only America could be galvanized into implementing its professed principles of democracy, how much it could nourish the impulses of all men to practice the basic things we are supposed to be fighting for. Instead many men cringe in fear because, justifiably or not, they are certain that any variation from the norm of "white superiority" will cost them dear.

Thus the majority perpetrate the kind of ridiculous situations which George Goodman, a Negro college graduate and Red Cross worker in England, relates. Mr. Goodman tells of his first experience in establishing a Red Cross club in a British city, bitterly blitzed, where he encountered the inevitable product of ignorance and bad manners in the form of stories "that out-Remused the Uncle Remus stories."

The first came from the lips of the Lord Mayor, who was plainly perplexed. This fine old gentleman told me of the experience of his City-wide Hospitality Committee that had been formed when first they heard that American soldiers were coming. The first Americans this Committee met—a group of officers—listened attentively to its plans. When they heard the report, they very gravely informed the Committee they were bringing two armies, a white one and a black. The Lord Mayor said the Committee had not thought in terms of two armies, but inasmuch as they were both American and Allies, this did not seem to present a major problem in their planning. Then the officers went into detail. They suggested that no planning be done for the blacks because they were ignorant, uncouth, and savage; that it would be most unfortunate to confuse them with colonial troops because they were a much lower branch of the colored race, a group that had been picked up on the coast of Africa.

My only response to this strange story was to laugh heartily and tell the Lord Mayor the timing and details of the gentlemen were bad. That it was true we had been picked up on the coast of Africa—totally against our will. But all of this picking up had been consummated years ago—some of it as much as three hundred years ago—and in the interim we had stopped off long enough in America to help these gentlemen build a great nation before coming on to assist in England with World War II.

I can still see the twinkle in the Lord Mayor's eyes as he smiled his appreciation.

But the very funniest story I heard during my whole stay in England came from a Negro sergeant. He had been invited to dinner in a British home. He noticed that every chair to which he was directed had a cushion in it, though none of the other folk seemed to enjoy such a luxury. After dinner, when they were all returning to the library, he unconsciously moved toward a chair in which there was no cushion. Much to his surprise, this gesture created a mild panic within the family group. All three members rushed headlong with cushions toward the chair he was about to sit in, the young man of the family sliding it under him just in the nick of time. It was not till two months later, when the sergeant was much better acquainted with the family, that the deep dark secret was revealed. The head of the household had mentioned to a white American that he intended having an occasional Negro to dinner. He was advised that such a step was dangerous, but, if it was carried through, they ought to keep in mind that all Negroes had tails which made it impossible for them to sit in the ordinary hard-bottomed chair without first becoming extremely uncomfortable, then excited and dangerous. Hence the family had put cushions in all the chairs he sat in, and when he seemed intent on trying one that had no cushion, a small crisis developed.

From this ridiculous culmination of sub-Potomac provincialism it is an easy transition to other contradictions which become increasingly clear and convincing to those whose skepticism of the aims of the Allies is already well developed. An American Negro jazz musician, his wife, and their two daughters were caught in France when the Germans seized that country. Like other aliens, they were interned. As Americans they were accorded the same special considerations given other citizens of the United States until we entered the war. Even after that event the four were given slightly better treatment than white Americans because the Nazi line then was to capitalize, if possible, on any and every means of creating anti-American prejudice, even including racial concepts diametrically opposed to the Nazi concept that Negroes are subhuman and savage. But whatever the reason, the four American Negroes suffered no greater segregation, discrimination, or humiliation than others were forced to endure. But when after several years an exchange was effected, the four emerged from Nazi Germany to free America to be faced once again with the stigma and embarrassment of being barred from certain places because they were colored.

Similar was the experience of René Maran, Goncourt prize winner in the twenties for his novel *Batouala*. After France fell the Nazis attempted to use French colonials as cat's-paws to induce their fellow colonials to submit without resistance to German rule, an effort which failed abysmally. Roi Ottley recounted in *PM* how the French Academy in a gesture of defiance to the Nazis awarded Maran its grand prize for his novel *Bête de la Brousse*. Not to be outdone, the Germans used every possible means to seduce Maran into writing to urge his countrymen to accept the inevitability and the wisdom of subjection to the Nazis. After a few months the barring from restaurants and other public places of Negroes, along with Jews and other enemies of the Nazis, was relaxed in Paris and other cities of Nazi-controlled France. But Maran was not fooled. According to Ottley, he wrote only destructively subtle pieces to show that even with all its faults America afforded Negroes and other minorities a greater opportunity for freedom.

With Teutonic stubbornness the Germans apparently continued to butter up Maran with the belief that he would eventually succumb to their wiles. Such was still their hope when Paris once again was French. Maran had gone nearly every night with his wife, even during the German occupation of Paris, to a café near his home for the drink and conversation so beloved of Parisians. When Paris was freed they went to the same café to celebrate the return of freedom. As they sat at their accustomed table five American white soldiers rushed over to jostle them from their chairs, raining insult and abuse upon them. Bewildered, Mme. Maran told

Ottley how even during the Nazi occupation she had never been insulted nor had an unkind word been uttered to her, because she was French and her distinguished husband a French colonial.

And thus is posed the question of the vastly opposite poles of opinion on race which may determine America's future—the rational fulfillment of the concept of a land where neither race nor creed nor color shall determine a man's opportunity or the concept of a land where those same circumstances will fix the pattern of our national and international behavior. Our War and Navy departments have not yet faced the issues involved. They still play an opportunist game, yielding almost invariably to the lowest common denominator of racial bigotry. In the meantime many thousands of officers and enlisted men whose instincts are to treat their fellow men as fellow men hesitate because they fear that reprisals will come if they act as they believe they should.

Chapter Thirteen

———◆———

REPERCUSSIONS of greater or lesser degree upon several groups will develop out of the manner in which the racial question has been handled by the United States during the war. These will manifest themselves in all parts of the world during the months immediately after the armistice and in the years which follow.

Most direct, of course, will be the effect upon the Negro soldier himself. Taught from early childhood at home and in school the stirring traditions of the United States and, like his white fellow American, taught by every means of education and propaganda to admire those who fought for freedom, he had, however, become conditioned, on leaving school, to discrimination. World War II has immeasurably magnified the Negro's awareness of the disparity between the American profession and practice of democracy. He has learned to listen cynically to Winston Churchill's "blood, sweat, and tears" oratory while India remains enslaved, maligned by British propaganda, and its leaders jailed.

The news that the American Negro soldier has received from back home has been predominantly disheartening. He has heard through letters, newspaper clippings, and from more recent arrivals of the continuation of the humiliation, beating, and even killing of Negro soldiers in the South. While I was overseas, news came of the killing in cold blood of Private Edward Green, a Negro soldier from New York City, by a bus driver in Alexandria, Louisiana. Soon after came a report that the War Department had requested the Department of Justice to take action against Green's murderer, declaring that "considering the testimony of all the witnesses, and the circumstances surrounding the case, the conclusion is inescapable that there was no justification, moral or legal, for the slaying of Private Edward Green by Odell Lachnette." High hopes were raised that Lachnette would be punished and thus at least retard the succession of such assaults and murders. But the Department of Justice refused to act.

The vitriolic and continued attacks on Negroes on the floor of Congress by representatives like John E. Rankin, of Mississippi, and the complete silence of other members of both houses of Congress in the face of such attacks had an effect which need not be described upon men who were facing discomfort and death as soldiers on foreign soil to protect the form of government of which Negrophobes were beneficiaries.

The bitter fight of Southern representatives and senators, aided by Republicans, to destroy or emasculate the FEPC, the formation of vigilante groups such as the Ku Klux Klan and the Christian Americans, brought constant reminders to Negro soldiers of World War II of the lynching of Negro soldiers in Southern states immediately after World War I for the "crime" of returning home in the uniform in which they had fought in France.

When there is added to that the vigorous efforts of many white Americans to spread the poison of race hatred in other countries, even as the war against Hitler was being fought, one has no difficulty in understanding why the Negro veteran will return to America disillusioned and cynical. America has no one else but herself to blame for such a state of mind. Yet the Negro soldier's attitude is not one of defeatist disillusionment. The majority of Negro soldiers will return home convinced that whatever betterment of their lot is achieved must come largely through their own efforts. They will return determined to use those efforts to the utmost.

World War II has given to the Negro a sense of kinship with other colored—and also oppressed—peoples of the world. Where he has not thought through or informed himself on the racial angles of colonial policy and master-race theories, he senses that the struggle of the Negro in the United States is part and parcel of the struggle against imperialism and exploitation in India, China, Burma, Africa, the Philippines, Malaya, the West Indies, and South America. The Negro soldier is convinced that as time proceeds that identification of interests will spread even among some brown and yellow peoples who today refuse to see the connection between their exploitation by white nations and discrimination against the Negro in the United States.

Had it not been for an optimism which carried the Negro through the days of slavery and reconstruction in the United States, he would long since have been crushed. That same tough-fibered hope helps to maintain in Negroes today at least a remnant of faith. They find modest consolation in the non-segregated training of Negro officers in World War II in officer candidate schools and the resulting six thousand Negro officers, as contrasted with one sixth that number in World War I; in the slight lifting of the barriers to Negroes in the Air Corps, Navy, Coast Guard, and Marines; in the sending of Negro combat troops to Italian and

French fronts. But they realize that these modest gains were obtained only through long and continuous struggle by the Negro himself. This the Negro soldier knows: that though he had to fight for the right to fight, and that after the war is over he will be forced to continue the struggle, he will return ready and determined to work for his freedom as never before. The winning by his organizations of such victories as the Texas White Primary Decision in the United States Supreme Court has strengthened his faith and taught him the need of organized effort. He knows that unemployment and possible depression face the returning white veteran, particularly in light of the trend toward reaction in Congress; he knows that his difficulties will be infinitely greater than those of his white fellow soldiers.

If the consequences of race prejudice were confined solely to American Negroes, however, they would constitute no serious problem for the United States which could not be handled after a fashion by repressive legislation and physical force against a troublesome minority. But it may well be proved that the effect upon the American Negro will be one of the most minor results. It has already been seen how the British Government made concessions in its official attitude toward the racial practices of some white American soldiers. In making such concessions, however, England has not improved its standing with many of its colored colonials. London correspondents of Indian, South African, West Indian, and other newspapers published in the British colonies have manifested a very considerable interest in the handling of the new racial problems created in England by Americans. British public opinion itself has not been untouched either. On numerous occasions mistreatment of American Negro soldiers and the introduction of racial discrimination in pubs, hotels, and other places of public accommodation have been discussed in Parliament. Widespread indignation has repeatedly been created by courts-martial of Negro soldiers which the British believed had been unjust or unduly harsh against Negro defendants. The results have been a marked increase in skepticism even among British people regarding the official government attitude on race questions. And there has been created among the so-called common men and women of England a distinct aversion to white American soldiers, created by the intolerance of a minority, which even the decent behavior of the majority has not been able to offset. "Two men having a friendly drink together in a pub is not news; a man objecting to the presence of another is, and creates headlines," Major Ralph Ingersoll wisely observed in commenting upon the unfortunate impression on the British people which has been created.

In the struggle between the United States and Great Britain for markets, air routes, and other advantages after the war there will be an inevitable weakening of the bonds forged by war. Resentment over one issue could be rationalized in criticism over a totally different one. Thus race prejudice and the memories of racial misbehavior by Americans have already become a part of the British concept of Americans, adding to the chasm between the two great English-speaking peoples. Particularly will this be true when legitimate American criticism of British colonial policy in India or Africa is voiced.

The soldiers of Canada, New Zealand, and, strangely enough—in light of her laws forbidding admission to that island of any but whites—Australia will take home with them from European and other battle fronts greatly augmented suspicion and mistrust against the United States because of her treatment of Negro soldiers. This has been created not only by resentment of the mistreatment of Negroes; it is even more due to the belief that Canadians, New Zealanders, Australians, Indians, and other dominion or colonial troops are almost invariably assigned to sections of battle fronts when casualties are high, with British and American troops replacing them near the time of victory. America's generosity, idealism, and heroism are being immeasurably diminished by these resentments.

Finally, the evil effect of misbehavior by a minority and the timorousness of the American Government in meeting such misbehavior will cost America and other white nations dearly so far as colored peoples, constituting two thirds of the earth's population, are concerned. Winston Churchill's recent statement that, as the war nears its end, ideology is being forgotten increasingly means to colored peoples that idealism is being conveniently shelved. Colored peoples, particularly in the Pacific, believed, whether correctly or not, that in its later stages the war was being fought to restore empire to Great Britain, France, Holland, and Portugal. The immediate resumption of control of Hollandia and other sections of Dutch New Guinea by the Dutch, and similar action by the British in Guadalcanal and Tarawa as soon as the Japanese had been driven out, the preparations being made by France to take over again control of Indo-China the minute the Nipponese are ejected, created increasing skepticism of the Allies throughout the Pacific.

Any person of normal intelligence could have foreseen this. With considerable effectiveness, the Japanese by radio and other means have industriously spread in the Pacific stories of lynchings, of segregation and discrimination against the Negro in the American Army, and of race riots in Detroit, Philadelphia, and other American cities. To each of these recitals has been appended the statement that such treatment of a colored minority in the United States is certain to be that given to brown and yellow peoples in the Pacific if the Allies, instead of the Japanese, win the war. No one can accurately estimate at this time the effectiveness of such propaganda. But it is certain that it has had wide circulation and has been believed by many. Particularly damaging has been the circulation of reports of clashes between white and Negro soldiers in the European and other theaters of operation.

Indissolubly tied in with the carrying overseas of prejudice against the Negro is the racial and imperialist question in the Pacific of Great Britain's and our intentions toward India and China. Publication of Ambassador William Phillips' blunt warning to President Roosevelt in May 1944 that India is a problem of the United States as well as of England despite British opposition to American intervention is of the highest significance. It reaffirmed warnings to the Western world by Wendell Willkie, Sumner Welles, Pearl Buck, and Henry Wallace, among others, that grave peril which might bring disaster to the entire world was involved in continued refusal to recognize the just claims for justice and equality by the colored people, particularly in the Orient. These people are not as powerless as some naïve Americans believe them to be. In the first place they have the strength of numbers, unified by resentment against the condescension and exploitation by white nations which Pearl Buck calls "the suppression of human rights to a degree which has not been matched in its ruthlessness outside of fascist-owned Europe," which can and possibly will grow into open revolt. The trend of such awakening and revolution is clearly to be seen in the demand which was made by China at the Dumbarton Oaks Conference of August 1944 that the Allied nations unequivocally declare themselves for complete racial equality. It is to be seen in Ambassador

Phillips' warning that though there are four million Indians under arms they are wholly a mercenary army whose allegiance to the Allies will last only as long as they are paid; and in his further revelation that all of these as well as African troops must be used to police other Indians instead of fighting Japan.

Permit me to cite a few solemn warnings of the inevitability of world-wide racial conflict unless the white nations of the earth do an about-face on the issue of race. "Moreover, during the years between 1920 and 1940 a period in the history of the Asiatic and Pacific peoples was in any event drawing to its close," says Sumner Welles, former Undersecretary of State, in his epochal book, *The Time for Decision*.

The startling development of Japan as a world power, and the slower but nevertheless steady emergence of China as a full member of the family of nations, together with the growth of popular institutions among many other peoples of Asia, notably India, all combined to erase very swiftly indeed the fetish of white supremacy cultivated by the big colonial powers during the nineteenth century. The thesis of white supremacy could only exist so long as the white race actually proved to be supreme. The nature of the defeats suffered by the Western nations in 1942 dealt the final blow to any concept of white supremacy which still remained.

While there are British and Dutch colonial administrators who show a "spirit of devotion, of decency and of self-abnegation," Mr. Welles remarks, there also are "yet only too many British representatives in the Far East [who] have demonstrated that type of thinking which is so well exemplified in the words of a high British official in India at the outset of the present century when he expressed a conviction which he asserted 'was shared by every Englishman in

India, from the highest to the lowest . . . the conviction in every man that he belongs to a race whom God has destined to govern and subdue.' "

The distinguished former Undersecretary might well have gone on to point out that had not the Russians and Chinese performed miracles of military offense and defense in World War II, or had not the black Governor-General of French Equatorial Africa, Félix Eboué, retained faith in the democratic process when white Frenchmen lost theirs, the so-called Anglo-Saxon nations and peoples would surely have lost this war. And Mr. Welles could have reminded his readers that brown and yellow peoples in Asia and the Pacific and black peoples in Africa and the West Indies and the United States are not ignorant of the truth that the war was won by men and women—white, yellow, black, and brown. Resumption of white arrogance and domination in the face of such facts may be disastrous to the peace of the world.

The distinguished novelist, Pearl Buck, hits hard on the same issue in her *American Unity and Asia* in the chapter ominously captioned, "Tinder for Tomorrow."[1]

The Japanese weapon of racial propaganda in Asia is beginning to show signs of effectiveness [she declares]. This is not because of peculiar skill in the way it is being used, but because it is being presented to persons who have had unfortunate experiences with English and American people. . . . It will be better for us if we acknowledge the danger in this Japanese propaganda. The truth is that the white man in the Far East has too often behaved without wisdom or justice to his fellow man. It is worse than folly—it is dangerous today—not to recognize the truth, for in it lies the tinder for tomorrow. Who of

[1]From *American Unity and Asia*, copyright, 1942, by Pearl S. Buck; published by the John Day Company, Inc.; and reprinted by arrangement with the author's agent, David Lloyd.

us can doubt it who has seen a white policeman beat a Chinese coolie in Shanghai, a white sailor kick a Japanese in Kobe, an English captain lash out with his whip at an Indian vendor—who of us, having seen such oriental sights or heard the common contemptuous talk of the white man in any colored country, can forget the fearful bitter hatred in the colored face and the blaze in the dark eyes?

Miss Buck tells how such stupid cruelty is put to use by the Japanese among the one billion colored people of the Pacific.

Race prejudice continues unabated among white people today, the Japanese are saying. Tokyo radio programs daily send their broadcasts over Asia in their campaign to drive out the white man. They dwell upon white exploitation of colored troops and cite mistreatment of Filipinos by the American military and similar treatment of Indian troops by the English. . . . "The colored peoples," Japanese propaganda says over and over again in a thousand forms, "have no hope of justice and equality from the white peoples because of their unalterable race prejudice against us." . . . The effect therefore of this Japanese propaganda cannot be lightly dismissed. It lies uneasy in the minds and memories of many at this moment who are loyally allied with Britain and the United States, in the minds and memories of colored peoples of Asia. Yes, and it lies uneasy, too, in the minds and memories of many colored citizens of the United States, who cannot deny the charge and must remain loyal in spite of it. For such minds realize that, though Nazism may give them nothing but death, yet the United States and Britain have given them too little for life in the past and not even promises for the future. Our colored allies proceed to war against the Axis not deceived or in ignorance. They know that it may not be the end of the war for them even when Hitler has gone down and Nazism is crushed and Japan returned to her isles again. The colored peoples know that for them the war for freedom may have to go on against the very white men at whose side they are now fighting.

These are grim words not pleasant to the ears of white America and Britain, who believe that the last shot fired in this war will mean the complete restoration of the way of life which preceded it. But the consequences of denying or ignoring them are solemnly voiced by an Englishman, Harold J. Laski, who bluntly warns that "Englishmen who put imperial power before social justice, Americans who think the color of a man's skin determines his rights—these are only some of the elements in our midst who might easily pervert the great victory into an epoch barren and ugly."

Will the United States after the war perpetuate its racial-discrimination policies and beliefs at home and abroad as it did during the war? Will it continue to follow blindly the dangerous and vicious philosophy voiced in Kipling's poem, *The White Man's Burden*, which Paul Hutchinson characterized in *World Revolution and Religion* as "the most significant cultural expression of the nineteenth century: even more significant than Nietzsche's discovery of the "*Übermensch*"? Will decent and intelligent America continue to permit itself to be led by the nose by demagogues and professional race-hate mongers—to have its thinking and action determined on this global and explosive issue by the lowest common denominator of public opinion?

Or will the United States, having found that prejudice is an expensive luxury, slough off the mistakes of the past and chart a new course both at home and in its relations with the rest of the world? Miss Buck supplies one answer:

This also the Far Eastern Allies are asking. Japan is busily declaring that we cannot. She is declaring in the Philippines, in China, in India, Malaya, and even Russia that there is no basis for hope that colored peoples can expect any justice from the people who rule in the United States, namely, the white people. For specific proof the Japanese point to our treatment of our own colored people, citizens of generations in the United States. Every lynching, every race riot, gives joy to Japan. The discriminations of the American army and navy and air forces against colored soldiers and sailors, the exclusion of colored labor in our defense industries and trade unions, all our social discriminations, are of the greatest aid today to our enemy in Asia, Japan. "Look at America," Japan is saying to millions of listening ears. "Will white Americans give you equality?"

Who can reply with a clear affirmative? The persistent refusal of Americans to see the connection between the colored American and the colored peoples abroad, the continued, and it seems even willful, ignorance which will not investigate the connection, are agony to those loyal and anxious Americans who know all too well the dangerous possibilities.

Is Japan right in what she says to Asia and the Pacific? And whether right or not, what effect is her propaganda—unhappily based largely on truth—having upon hundreds of millions of people in what were once far places but today are but a few hours away from New York or Washington or San Francisco? Upon people whose good will and faith in our integrity are vital to our own national security?

During the middle stages of the war I made a study of Japanese radio and other propaganda among the people of the Orient and of German propaganda, almost invariably identical in language and content to the Japanese, in Latin America and Africa. Every lynching, every race riot like the one in Detroit in 1943 and the one in Philadelphia in 1944 against employment of qualified Negroes on streetcars, every killing or other mistreatment of a Negro soldier in a Southern training camp or city, every anti-Negro diatribe on the floor of Congress, every refusal to abolish racial segregation in the armed services of the United States was played up over and over again. Significantly enough, there was little embellishment of the details, probably because little was needed. In one form or another this moral was driven home: See what the United States does to its own colored people; this is the way you colored people of the world will be treated if the Allied nations win the war! Be smart and cast your lot with another colored people, the Japanese, who will never mistreat fellow colored people!

What will America's answer be? If already planned race riots and lynchings of returning Negro soldiers "to teach them their place" are consummated, if Negro war workers are first fired, if India remains enslaved, if Eboué's people go back to disease and poverty to provide luxury and ease for Parisian boulevardiers, World War III will be in the making before the last gun is fired in World War II. In *One World*, Wendell Willkie reported that "everywhere I found polite but skeptical people, who met my questions about their problems and difficulties with polite but ironic questions about our own. The maladjustments of races in America came up frequently." Such skepticism is but beginning. The question is posed bluntly: Can the United States, Britain, and other "white" nations any longer afford, in enlightened self-interest, racial superiority?

What to do?

The United States, Great Britain, France, and other Allied nations must choose without delay one of two courses—to revolutionize their racial concepts and practices, to abolish imperialism and grant full equality to all of its people, or else prepare for World War III. Another Versailles Treaty providing for "mandates," "protectorates," and other devices for white domination will make such a war inevitable. One of the chief deterrents will be Russia. Distrustful of Anglo-American control of Europe, many and perhaps all of the Balkan states may through choice or necessity ally themselves with Russia. If Anglo-Saxon practices in China and India are not drastically and immediately revised, it is probable and perhaps certain that the people of India, China, Burma, Malaya, and other parts of the Pacific may also move into the Russian orbit as the lesser of two dangers.

As for the United States, the storm signals are unmistakable. She can choose between a policy of appeasement of bigots—which course she gives every indication now of following—and thus court disaster. Or she can live up to her ideals and thereby both save herself and help to avert an early and more disastrous resumption of war.

A wind *is* rising—a wind of determination by the have-nots of the world to share the benefits of freedom and prosperity which the haves of the earth have tried to keep exclusively for themselves. That wind blows all over the world. Whether that wind develops into a hurricane is a decision which we must make now and in the days when we form the peace.